Education
and deprivation

In series with this book
The teacher in a changing society

Forthcoming
The education of the professions
Aspects of the curriculum
The circumstance of learning

Education
and deprivation

Edited by   JAMES RUSHTON, B.Sc., M.Ed., Ph.D.
Deputy Director, Colleges of Education Division, Faculty of
Education, University of Manchester

JOHN D. TURNER, M.A.
Professor of Education and Director, Colleges of Education
Division, Faculty of Education, University of Manchester

Manchester University Press

41516

Published by Manchester University Press
Oxford Road, Manchester M13 9PL

ISBN 0 7190 0624 4

Printed in Great Britain
by William Clowes & Sons Limited
London, Colchester and Beccles

Contents

Preface   *page*   vi

1 Education and deprivation: an introduction JAMES RUSHTON
Deputy Director, Colleges of Education Division, Faculty of
Education, University of Manchester   1

*2 Parents' attitudes to education and their consequences for
working-class children* JOHN BYNNER
Senior Lecturer in Education, Faculty of Educational
Studies, Open University   7

3 Attainment, environment and education ERIC BATTEN
Lecturer in Education, Faculty of Education, University of
Manchester   23

4 Educational Priority Areas A. H. HALSEY
Director, Department of Social and Administrative Studies,
University of Oxford   46

*5 Towards a solution of the EPA problem: the community
school* ERIC MIDWINTER
formerly Director of Priority; Director, Liverpool Teachers'
Centre   58

*6 The performance of children from ethnic minority
backgrounds in primary schools* A. N. LITTLE
Director of Reference and Technical Services, Community
Relations Commission   71

Bibliography   102

Author index   105

Preface

The subject of education and deprivation is an important one for the community. Many of the ills of society are closely connected with it. It was rather optimistically thought less than two decades ago that education was the vehicle by which social, cultural and emotional deprivation could be countered. Now recent work by Halsey (1972) and Jencks (1972) leads to the conclusion that the ills of society are too fundamental for educators alone to be able to make very much impact.

Halsey and Jencks see the solutions as being contained in political and economic change and as such out of the reach of education to some extent. For classroom teachers, college and university lecturers this would suggest that child minding was their role instead of educating. At the very least educators would be demotivated by the claims of the researchers, however forward-looking they might be. The arguments in this book could help the reader to decide whether such claims have any substance.

The book contains much material which should help the educator in his task with deprived pupils or students as well as expositions of the research. It is the result of a series of public lectures delivered in the School of Education at the University of Manchester late in the autumn term of 1973. The audience was particularly full on each occasion and the lectures stimulated much far-reaching, interesting and sometimes heated debate. It is hoped that the book will have a similar effect in stimulating a wider circle of readers.

Thanks are due to the lecturers and to their chairman, Mr J. Barnes, Professor F. Musgrove and Mrs A. Nicholls.

J.R.
J.D.T.

1

J. RUSHTON *Education and deprivation: an introduction*

Deprivation for the purpose of this chapter will be taken to mean the lack of an adequate preparation, either cultural or social, which places a pupil at a disadvantage when compared with his peer group. The particular point of reference by which the deprivation will be judged is that of the British school system. If a pupil, because of family background, inadequate peer or reference group support or adverse financial or economic circumstances, is unable to take full advantage of the educational system in any of its myriad forms he or she can be said to be suffering some form of deprivation from an educational point of view. One of the difficulties in framing this definition is that the educational system is immensely varied in form and type throughout the British Isles. In spite of this variety certain features tend to be common to all schools and systems.

1   Pupils are separated into age groups and roughly into equivalent achievement groups, usually within subjects.
2   Cumulative records are kept, in a variety of ways, of the pupils' performance in academic subjects and often on some measures of social skill.
3   The basis of the teaching tends to be intellectual in focus, with an emphasis on verbal skill.

Thus when the question of deprivation is looked at the three factors mentioned above are the background against which it is placed. Pupils who enter this school system suffering social or cultural deprivation are in danger of having their deprivation exaggerated rather than ameliorated. Schools have to cater for all their intake as well as the deprived. This forces them to assign priorities to their resources and to teach where the incremental gain in terms of intellectual or social skill is at its highest. Attempts are made in almost all good schools to counteract the effect of these conditions—remedial classes, smaller groups for backward children, the provision of many forms of pastoral care—but at the end of the line the pupils who entered the school from a deprived social or cultural background tend to be the ones who have gained least.

Education is taken to be a continuous process which starts at birth and finishes at death. A person is educating himself or being educated during the whole of it. The agencies through which the education is gained are the home, the family, the school and the peer group. Much deprivation is evident when children enter a school situation because of inadequate home or family background. Some of the characteristics of this deprivation as analysed by Lewis (1966) and Will and Vatter (1965) are a sense of low status, lack of power, cultural alienation, economic deprivation and limited opportunity. It is this situation which faces the school when children present themselves for education.

The schools themselves have value systems which vary from the overt and well documented to the covert and implicit. The value systems tend to favour the middle-class child from a home in which there is sufficient financial support for books, study facilities and other physical attributes, and in which a varied and interesting social life is provided. Many working-class pupils—though not all—feel left out of the system in school because they lack one or more of the above facilities. These pupils can be said to be deprived and are in some danger of failing to benefit from the positive aspects of education. If children enter the system from a social or cultural background which is different from or alien to that of the school they are at an immediate disadvantage. As they progress through the system from infant school to junior school and then to secondary school their disadvantage tends to worsen, owing to the greater emphasis which is placed on intellectual learning and the acquisition of academic knowledge as pupils ascend the ladder of formal schooling. Hence the great feeling of relief with which educators have greeted the recent emphasis on nursery education in terms of resources and finance. This is seen as a small, inadequate but perceptible step in the direction of redressing the disadvantage which many children suffer from being born into a deprived home background. But there is no certainty that the increased nursery provision will attract the child from the deprived home. There is a definite danger that the alert mother from the adequate or more than adequate home will take further advantage of these increased facilities to the detriment of the deprived in times of financial stringency. Almost by definition families from deprived home backgrounds are unable or unwilling to seek the advantages which nursery education can provide for their children.

Lest this chapter should sound depressingly like the philosophy of doom it should be stated that there are ways in which disadvantage or deprivation may be diagnosed, and steps which may then be taken to try to alleviate it in the early stages before children enter formal schooling. Social and welfare workers could add disadvantage or deprivation to their list of danger signals to be spotted and use their persuasive powers to have children placed in nursery schools with an environment which will help them to adjust easily to formal schooling. Bereiter and Engleman (1960) have written controversially about their view of how the curriculum of pre-schools should be structured for children from deprived home backgrounds. They advocate formal teaching and lesson organisation as being more effective on the grounds that this is what such children have missed at home. There are numerous studies showing that children who enter school after having made a start on the basic skills of reading have less trouble in settling into formal schooling and also achieve better than those who do not possess such skills on entry. One such study is that by Kellmer-Pringle et al. (1966). There is a growing feeling, though, that an imposed solution by official persons such as social or welfare workers is less effective than that of re-educating the home into adopting the *mores* of non-deprived homes. Eric Midwinter's chapter in this book contains details of schemes which have been tried and tested in this respect. Hall (1974) has commented on the effects on backward readers of educating the home through the mother to give support to the child. In his study the permanent gains were made by children from homes where the mother had been trained to support the child in reading skills.

So there is some evidence that the problem of deprivation in the home and its effect on education could best be alleviated by effecting changes in the behaviour of the families from which children come. The school would then be presented with a pupil whose value systems were nearer to its own. However, this is a long-term aim which may or may not be realised. The problem of how to deal with the disadvantaged child when he presents himself, however reluctantly, is still firmly with the school. There are many well formulated systems for treating academic backwardness—by teaching in smaller groups or individually, by providing expert attention and teaching, by the provision of adequate and expertly constructed teaching aids, by the provision of financial support for social events such as school camps and trips and by adequate, expert and caring pastoral provision. But the problem is deeper than treating academic failure. It is one of creating a sufficiently sympathetic, supportive and welcoming atmosphere into which a pupil can enter.

The school is to some extent dealing with an interface situation in which the values and attitudes of the disadvantaged home or group are placed in opposition to those of the school. The school cannot change its position unequivocally to any great extent. If it did it might be that the disadvantaged or deprived groups would then be those who were previously advantaged, and in almost every case they would be more numerous. The school has therefore to create a situation in which the value system of the disadvantaged can be allowed to change without threat. Or—if it is impossible to change it—that the child should feel as if it is entering a tolerant environment in which coexistence is possible. In this regard the provision in the classroom situation of supportive people in the form of teachers, auxiliaries or other pupils could be of great benefit to the socially disadvantaged. Team teaching for certain parts of the curriculum is often helpful in this respect. It must be stressed, however, that the teacher should be in a liberal management position with the others in his classroom. It is also suggested that this support should be provided in addition to a thorough training in cognitive skills and not at the expense of it. Rushton and Young (1974) showed that the writing of working-class adolescents is in some instances as elaborate and vital in code as that of public school boys, and they advocate a more enlightened attitude to the teaching of English to working-class boys. This is in contrast to the somewhat gloomy analysis of the language abilities of working-class boys by Bernstein (1961), which is widely accepted by teachers. In his chapter in this book John Bynner draws attention to the disillusion which the parents of working-class children experience in their contacts with school. When their children start, many working-class parents make contact with the primary school. But at the secondary school stage the number is woefully diminished. Secondary schools have a task to perform in enabling the parents of working-class children to understand the syllabus their children are studying. It may be that a more open attitude about the content and method of classroom teaching would help the disadvantaged pupil in secondary schools. Organising open days is too naive a solution to put forward, since they are generally rejected by the parents of deprived children. A more supportive, tolerant and understanding role would seem to be necessary if better and longer-lasting contacts between parents and school are to grow. The involvement of parents of children from a deprived environment would appear to be essential if they are to subscribe to the values which the schools tend to hold about education. As Swift (1966) points out, very few working-class parents subscribe to the view that education is valuable for its own sake. This in spite of the findings of Jencks (1972), who points out that, however inappropriate the school may be in almost every way possible, length of stay has a positive influence on job status and economic gain. The writer fears, however, that the findings of Jencks and others will not reach the audience who would benefit most from reading them and understanding their significance. They are caught up in the rejection situation, in which most formal education is merely tolerated by the disadvantaged or deprived. This emphasises the need for adequate communication systems to be used by schools, social and welfare workers in their contacts with the product of deprived homes.

Eric Midwinter and A. H. Halsey see the solution to some of the problems of deprivation as the formation of community schools—schools in which most persons in the community have a stake and in which they not only have a stake but play an active part. Some of the ways in which such schools can operate and, it is hoped, make inroads into the vast problem of the incongruity of values and attitudes of the parents of children from deprived backgrounds and those of the school are well documented in their respective chapters in this book. Nevertheless community schools are not yet the norm, nor are they likely to become so quickly. In the short term traditional schools are the agencies through which any breakthrough to the disadvantaged will have to be made. In these schools attitudes will necessarily have to become more flexible in the first instance so that their values can be seen as more worthwhile and less threatening to that section of society which tends to reject them.

It will be noted that this chapter has concentrated on the problem of deprivation and education in normal schools. It has also concentrated on children who are living in entire but deprived homes. No attempt has been made to examine the problems of deprivation as they apply to children who for one reason or another live in institutions. The attention of the reader is directed to the work of Donnison (1972), where the effects of such extreme deprivation are adequately chronicled.

2

J. BYNNER *Parents' attitudes to education and their consequences for working-class children*

Ever since Floud, Halsey and Martin (1957) demonstrated that secondary selection is strongly biased in favour of the middle class, people have tried to unravel the features of family background that enhance or hinder a child's educational prospects. The major longitudinal studies carried out by Douglas for the Population Investigation Committee (1964) and by Kellmer Pringle for the National Child Development Committee (1966) have reinforced the earlier findings. They have shown that children's performance on tests of educational attainment are strongly related to social class differences. And these differences become apparent soon after entry into primary school. The middle-class home appears to be in tune with the demands the school places on the growing child; the working-class home appears to be discordant with them. Once the stage is set, the child retains his position on it. Though the gap may not get much wider as children's educational careers proceed, its consequences for working-class children are manifested right up to the end. Working-class children leave school *earlier* and take *fewer* examinations than their middle-class contemporaries of comparable ability. Perhaps, as Douglas hints, part of this wastage of educational talent is a product of the *expectations* of academic failure fostered among working-class children in the primary school (1968). The importance of these expectations on the part of pupils *and teachers* cannot be overestimated. In a recent book, *Teachers' Expectations and Pupil Performance*, Pidgeon (1970) presents strong evidence to suggest that the beliefs teachers hold about a child's capabilities can inhibit the child's educational performance. Children who stay on in the lower streams of primary school do better on objective tests than those of the *same* age and ability who go on to secondary school.

But what exactly is it in the working-class home that sets a child off so early in life to a less exalted school career than he deserves? And why is it that many working-class children surmount the obstacles that apparently lie before them? The limitations of an educational prescription based solely on social class were demonstrated in the work carried out by G. F. Peaker for the Plowden committee (1967). As is well known, he showed that the most important set of influences on children's educational achievement is their parents' attitudes to education. In Peaker's study two-thirds of the variation in educational attainment between the primary schools he surveyed could be attributed to this source. The qualities of the schools themselves appeared to make only a small contribution. In other words, educational disadvantage is not simply dependent on social status but represents a whole syndrome of family characteristics of which the most important are the parents' attitudes. Parents who aspire to the goals schools set for their children, and who actively involve themselves in the educational process, substantially improve their children's prospects. Other parents who reject these goals and perhaps through no fault of their own, provide little educational support for their children lay the foundations of educational failure.

Some sociologists have criticised Peaker's conclusions on the grounds that the various indicators of parents' attitudes to education which he employed in his analysis are themselves a manifestation of social class differences, and until the basic socio-economic divisions in society disappear working-class children will remain at a disadvantage (Peters, 1969). Others have gone further, arguing that the educational system is itself at fault; it should attempt to match working-class parents' aspirations and values rather than try to change them (Halsey, 1972).

Whatever the merits of these arguments, much of what Peaker

describes as parents' attitudes does seem amenable to change. Only a quarter of the variation in the attitudes he investigated could be attributed to such fixed features of the home environment as parents' occupation, income level and educational experience. Thus a strong element of educational disadvantage is, to use Peaker's word, 'malleable'. If at least *one* goal of primary education is agreed to be the transmission of the basic skills of literacy and numeracy to children, then educational policies directed at changing parents' attitudes are likely to produce an improvement. This, of course, underlies the strategy of much of the Plowden committee's EPA proposals. The community school in which common goals and means of achieving them can be worked out between teachers and parents may be seen as a medium for attitude change.

The trouble is that such schools are still relatively rare, and in the school system as a whole there is little evidence to suggest that much attempt is made to enhance the opportunities of the deprived sections of the school community. As I shall try to show in this chapter, the indications are that as children proceed through the educational system those from the poorest backgrounds become increasingly alienated from it. As school experience increases positive attitudes to education decline.

The evidence for this point of view comes from data collected from parents' interviews in the original Plowden survey (Morton-Williams, 1967) and the follow-up work which I carried out four years later (Bynner, 1972). At the follow-up stage two-thirds of the 3,000 children in the Plowden survey had reached secondary school—the first and fourth years respectively. The remaining group had reached the top year of primary school.

The parents' interviews covered a wide range of topics, including the parents' aspirations for their children and the ways in which they were helping the children to achieve them. What I am going to do is look at some of the changes which occur in these characteristics over the period from primary to secondary school. I am going to examine particularly differences between social classes and between different types of secondary school. I shall look first at parents' aspirations and then move on to those other attitudinal characteristics which may be looked upon as indicators of parental alienation from the educational system. Attitudes in this study are assessed both from the opinions expressed by parents *and* their behaviour in relation to education. Social class definitions are based on the Registrar General's classification of the head of household's occupation.

Parental aspirations

The survey data suggest that schools have been remarkably successful in encouraging parents to have high aspirations for their children. At primary school most parents set their sights on a grammar school place for their child. Most of them also hope their child will stay on at school, take examinations and get a non-manual job. But opportunities for achieving these aims are often severely limited—particularly among the manual occupational groups. Let us see what happens at primary school.

We often hear about the importance of giving parents choice in secondary education. What many of its advocates overlook is that in a selective system there are limited opportunities for parents' preferences to be met. About two-thirds of the parents in the original Plowden survey said they hoped their child would get into a grammar school; only a quarter succeeded in doing so. As might be expected, some sections of the population do better than others in this respect. Figure 2.1 shows the proportions of parents in each occupational class who said they hoped their child would get into a grammar school. Clearly this is the aim of many more middle-class than working-class parents; but substantial proportions of working-class parents do subscribe to it. When we look at the proportions whose children actually succeed in gaining grammar school entrance, then we see where the disappointment is greatest. Nearly two-thirds of the professional group of parents had succeeded in getting their children into grammar schools, in comparison with only 7 per cent of the unskilled group.

The most immediate effect of the failure of working-class parents to achieve their ambitions for their children when they were at primary school is a dampening of aspirations at the secondary stage. This is evident from the attitudes they express towards the age at which their child will leave school. When their children were at

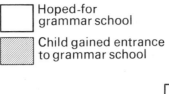

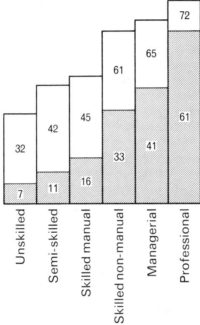

'FIG. 2.1. Grammar school entrance: parents' hopes and actual attendance (%)

primary school most working-class parents in the study shared the aim of middle-class parents in wanting their children to stay on at school beyond the minimum age. At secondary school the gap between the two classes widens dramatically (fig. 2.2). Although the same proportion of middle-class parents want their child to stay on at school, among the working-class parents there is a marked decline. For example, among the unskilled group the proportion falls from two-thirds when the children were at primary school to below half when they had reached secondary school.

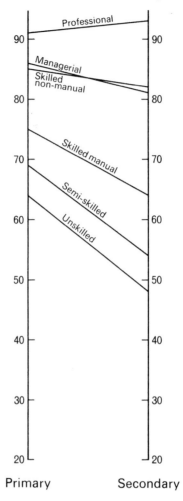

FIG. 2.2, Desire for child to leave school above the minimum age (%)

Another side of this picture is shown by attitudes to education beyond the age of eighteen (fig. 2.3). I think it is particularly striking that in relation to this aim middle-class hopes actually rise from primary to secondary school. Among the working class there is

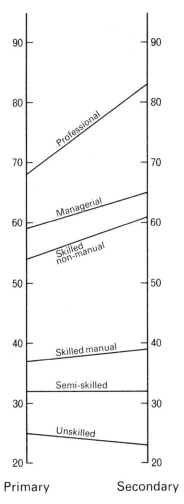

FIG. 2.3. Desire for child to go on studying beyond the age of eighteen (%)

barely any change. From these findings it is difficult to escape the conclusion that middle-class parents seem to be gaining *more* from the educational system as their children proceed through it. In contrast, working-class children seem to *lose out* in it.

Obviously the ambitions parents hold for their children are dependent to a certain extent on the type of secondary school their children gain entry to. In secondary modern schools, which contain the highest proportion of working-class children, opportunities for continuing education are most limited. It is all the more significant, therefore, that sizeable numbers of parents with children at secondary modern schools continue to subscribe to educational aims. About 40 per cent said they hoped their children would take GCE examinations and, perhaps more surprisingly, three-quarters wanted their child to get a non-manual job. As might be expected, in the grammar schools at the other end of the scale virtually *all* parents had these aims for their children. In addition, about two-thirds of this group wanted their child to go on to university or teacher training college. Once again middle-class parents seem to be in a good position to realise their hopes; working-class parents seem set for further disappointments.

Parental alienation

The failure of so many working-class parents to achieve their ambitions for their children probably lays the foundations for the alienation from the educational system which many of them clearly feel. This may be exacerbated by their inability to provide the educational support for their children that the school demands of them. It is useful to distinguish between two types of educational support which parents can give to their children. First, such fixed characteristics of the child's home background as his family's material prosperity and his parents' own educational experience may hinder or enhance his ability to study. Secondly, the steps his parents take to help him actively with his school work may exercise a strong influence on his educational progress.

Let us look at each of these features of home background in turn. It is well known that overcrowding is more common in working-class homes than in middle-class ones, and far fewer working-class parents have had extended educational experience. Similarly, when we look at the characteristics of children attending the different types of secondary school we see the same evidence of poor home backgrounds in the least privileged educational sector. To take just one example of the type of home circumstance which may inhibit the child from studying, substantially fewer secondary modern school parents than their grammar school counterparts said their children had a room of their own in which to study. Clearly the lack of this facility sets severe limitations on the children's ability to cope with school demands.

With respect to parents' own educational experience there is also a striking disparity between the secondary modern school and the grammar school. Perhaps the strongest manifestation of it is the extent to which the parents engage in reading activities. We constructed a scale to assess the general level of literacy in the home. This covered such items as membership of a library, interest in reading and evidence of books in the household. Only a third of the secondary modern parents gained an above-average score on this scale, in comparison with two-thirds of those with children at grammar schools.

One of the main ways parents can help their children educationally is by forging early contacts with the school. We asked the parents whether they had talked to the Head when the children first attended the current school. Here there is further evidence of increasing alienation from the school among working-class parents (fig. 2.4). Although, in company with middle-class parents, the majority had visited the Head of the primary school when their child first went there, far fewer had taken this step with the secondary school. On the other hand, among middle-class parents contacts of this kind increased. To take the two extremes, in comparison with the parents in the unskilled group twice the number of professional parents (80 per cent in all) had visited the Head of the secondary school.

Visiting the Head is, of course, only the first of many ways in which parents can become actively involved in their children's education. At primary school many parents, particularly in middle-class groups, go much further in reading to their children, helping them with school work and generally maintaining a high level of interest and involvement in what their children are doing at school. At secondary school, perhaps for reasons associated with the curriculum, there are indications that direct involvement of this kind in the children's education declines. But again it remains highest in the grammar schools. The one exception is a greater involvement of fathers in the education of their children as shown by visits to the school and in-

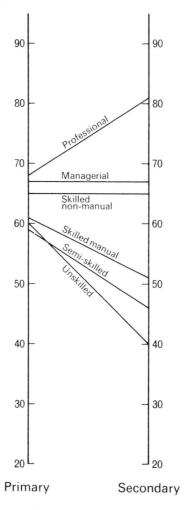

FIG. 2.4. Parents visited Head when child first entered present school (%)

terest in the child's progress. This increases from primary to secondary school and appears to be particularly strong among grammar school parents (fig. 2.5).

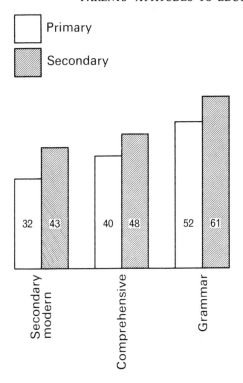

FIG. 2.5. Above-average score on paternal interest and support (%)

Obviously parents who have not had the benefit of extended education themselves are less well equipped to help the children with school work than with those who have had this advantage. This inadequacy puts an even greater responsibility on the schools. The trouble is that it is the very group of parents who appear to need help most that have the least contact with the school throughout the children's time there. Whether the parents visit the school depends, of course, on whether the school holds functions to which parents are invited. Here there are signs that the schools where contact between teachers and parents may be most needed do in fact provide the fewest opportunities for them. The parents reported that open days were held in about 60 per cent of the schools of all types that their children were attending. But only a *third* of the secondary modern schools appeared to hold *parent–teacher association* meetings in comparison with over *half* the grammar schools.

Holding functions for parents to attend gives no guarantee that they will attend them. Here the greater disaffection between the home and school among secondary modern parents is readily apparent. For example, two-thirds of the secondary modern school parents said they attended open days, in comparison with 90 per cent of the grammar school parents. Similarly, about a *third* of secondary modern parents attended the PTA meetings when they were held, in comparison with nearly *two-thirds* of grammar school parents. It is also worth noting

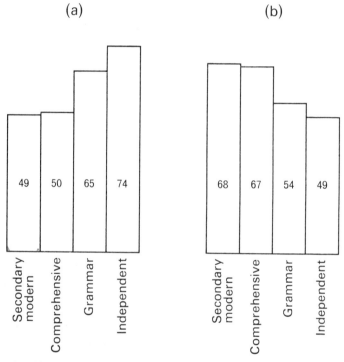

FIG. 2.6. (*a*) Above-average score on satisfaction with present school. (*b*) Above-average score on desire for greater parent–teacher communication. (All figures per cent.)

that, according to the parents of fourth-year children, careers meetings which might be expected to hold a special interest for the parents of children at secondary modern schools, were held in only a third.

These findings raise the question whether secondary modern schools do enough to encourage parents to visit the school or whether the parents are simply not interested. We gain some indication of the answer from parents' responses on two attitude scales to different aspects of the school. One of these scales measured the extent to which the parents felt generally *satisfied* with the school their children were attending. This covered such opinions as satisfaction with the child's progress, whether the parent wanted to be told more about the child's progress, and whether the parent considered the teachers to be equally interested in *all* the children. On this criterion parents in secondary modern schools and comprehensive schools were least satisfied with the school; those in grammar schools, and particularly independent schools, were most satisfied (fig. 2.6). The other side of the picture is shown by parents' scores on a scale which measured their desire for more parent–teacher communication. This covered such opinions as preferences for teachers to visit the home rather than for the parents to visit the school, and the view that teachers should ask parents more about their children. Parents' positions on this scale suggest an increasing desire for more information in the least academic types of school. It seems that independent schools are the most successful in meeting parents' needs in this respect; secondary modern schools are the least successful.

It might be argued that the dissatisfaction which many working-class parents feel with the school their children attend is a product of a lack of sympathy with its aims. This may be reflected, as Jackson and Marsden (1962) suggest, in a greater involvement on the part of the children in leisure activities outside the school.

There is some evidence for this. Although parents in all social classes appear to share similar beliefs about the need for the school to concern itself with the personal and moral development of their children, those in the working class are far less convinced of the value of school experience for its own sake. We constructed an attitude scale to assess the extent to which parents subscribed to this belief. The scale covered such beliefs as support for raising the school-leaving age, approval for girls staying on at school and approval of school uniform. Moving up the social classes there was a marked rise in the proportions of parents who obtained an above-average score on this attitude scale. Only a quarter of the unskilled group came high on the scale, in comparison with nearly two-thirds of the professional group.

This difference between the social classes reinforces the evidence of alienation from the school among many working-class parents. It may be the case, as Swift (1966) suggests, that even many of those with high aspirations see school simply as a means of achieving higher social status, but not as a valuable experience in its own right. This is reflected in other attitudes which working-class parents hold towards their children's involvement in leisure activities inside and outside the school. Working-class parents in the study were far *less* likely than middle-class parents to encourage their children to attend school clubs and societies, and far *more* of them approved of their children doing part-time jobs. (Only a fifth of the unskilled manual group disapproved of these, in comparison with half the professional group.) From the parents' accounts of their children's leisure activities the picture of working-class alienation from the school and its values is extended. Middle-class children bring books home to read, spend a lot of their time doing homework and rarely watch television. If they do go out it is to school clubs or societies or associations like Scouts and Guides outside the school. Working-class children, on the other hand, spend much more of their time watching television, doing housework and going out with friends. They spend far less time on clubs and societies. Thus again, like their parents, children at the upper end of the social class scale appear to be in harmony with the school. Those at the other end of the scale are out of step with it.

Conclusions

What does all this add up to for the prospects of working-class children in the educational system? We know from Peaker's work for the Plowden committee that parents' attitudes play perhaps the major part in the multitude of influences that determine school success. But why is it that they exercise such a decisive effect on a child's educational progress?

In a recent book, *Social Disadvantage and Educational Opportunity*, Kelsall and Kelsall (1971) draw attention to the attitudes children hold which are symptomatic of educational backwardness. They distinguish between attitudes which signify poor motivation and others which signify alienation from the school. The former is characterised by lack of incentive to strive for educational goals. The latter is identified with hostility towards the school engendered by the experience of failure there. It is not hard to see how these feelings may be transmitted by many working-class parents to their children. The series of disappointments which they experience at the hands of the educational system, coupled with their own inability to do anything to mitigate them, probably lie at the heart of the child's poor motivation and alienation from school.

At the end of the trail from a low stream in a poor primary school to a bad secondary school the alienation of the whole family from the educational system is complete.

Even those parents who do continue to strive for educational goals may be doing so almost despite school intentions. Swift (1966) argues that many of these parents use the school simply as a means of compensating for their own social and economic disadvantages. School provides, through their children, a route for improving their social status. Education as a means of enhancing the quality of life largely passes them by.

These conclusions are not particularly new; nor are the findings on which they are based a uniquely British phenomenon. In Denmark, for example, a recent follow-up survey of secondary school parents produced a virtually identical picture (Andersen and Hansen, 1972). But they do serve to highlight an important deficiency in our educational system. Wherever we look there seems to be a serious mismatch between educational provision and the needs of a substantial number of its clients. In a selective system of secondary education, grammar schools do by and large succeed in meeting parents' expectations. The other schools fail to do so.

Perhaps one ray of light in an otherwise bleak picture is the effect the growth of comprehensive education is having on it. Although, in terms of family background characteristics, children attending comprehensive schools seem very similar to those of secondary moderns, there is evidence of a rise in aspirations among the parents whose children attend such schools and a slightly greater all-round satisfaction with the school. Perhaps the neighbourhood comprehensive school can provide a more acceptable school environment for the children from the more deprived sections of the community. And this leads me to a final point about educational policy. The main plank of compensatory education strategy as proposed by such writers as Halsey (1972) and Chazan (1973) rests on the integration of the school into the community. This, of course, is directed at the primary stage of education—if the problems for children and parents are solved there then the rest will follow naturally.

Such a policy overlooks the point that the secondary school places quite different demands on the child. The secondary stage of education is the time when adulthood begins and decisions have to be made about jobs and further education. New pressures begin to be felt, such as those from the peer group. So schools have a particularly crucial role to play in enabling parents *and* children to achieve their goals. It is a cause for some concern, therefore, to find that the gulf between secondary schools and working-class parents is if anything wider than it is at primary school. Perhaps the answer is the extension of the compensatory education concept to the secondary stage. At the very least, greater recognition of the aspirations and needs of working-class parents may help to reduce the gap between them and the schools their children attend. Halsey (1972), in disputing the value of the liberal aim of equality of opportunity as an end in itself, makes a particularly telling point on this issue. 'They [the advocates of this aim] failed to notice that the major determinants of educational attainment were not school masters, but social situations, not curriculum, but motivation, not *formal* access to the school, but support in the family and the community.' The opening of school doors in the *fullest* sense is essential if any compensatory education programme is to succeed.

3

E. BATTEN *Attainment, environment and
education*

Although our appreciation of the complex relationships between environment, heredity and attainment has grown steadily through the last decade, and the universal and consistent variations by social class in the distribution of life chances in general and educational opportunities and attainments in particular are now documented beyond peradventure, there is little to suggest that there has been any significant attempt to come to grips with the implications for education of our increased knowledge.

My objectives in this paper are twofold: firstly to develop at some length those considerations which I see as attaching to the form of interpretation associated with environment–attainment analysis in this country. Especially I want to discuss the practice of categorising survey data as evidence of attitudes or material and socio-economic circumstance. In the course of this I shall refer particularly to the evidence drawn from the Plowden follow-up research conducted at Manchester (Ainsworth and Batten, 1974). My second objective is to discuss, somewhat more briefly, some difficulties attaching to the well-meaning practical proposals which resulted from such studies—difficulties which need to be considered when assessing the likely outcomes of the piecemeal proposals so far made. Especially I shall be concerned to outline some of the difficulties attaching to the closer development of home–school relations and the practical implementation of the community school concept at the secondary level of education (Plowden, 1967; Halsey, 1972; Midwinter, 1973).

Before dealing in detail with a specific review of the problems of categorising environmental data in terms of attitude and circumstance variables it may be of value if I state my general view of the consequence of such forms of analysis. In essence I take the view that the 'attitudinal' interpretations in the analysis of the association of environment with variations in educational attainment have led to the assumption that what is required is parental socialisation into the educational milieu; the creation of what Jean Floud (1962) once described as teacher missionaries, individuals who will proselytise for education until every family will qualify for the description of 'la famille éducogène' (1961). Such an assumption ignores the growing body of knowledge which consistently demonstrates the incapacity of education to compensate for the effects of the wider society (Jencks *et al.*, 1972), and which validates a similar assumption, made perhaps more instinctively by a large part of the population, that compulsory education has little relevance as a determinant of the future opportunities available for their children.

If this view is accepted, then strategies designed to motivate the closer attachment of parents and their children to an educational system which can *per se* only ever determine the advantage of a tiny minority seems to me to divert attention from what is, I believe, a more central educational consideration, which is: whether it is possible (the moral and political questions are avoided) to motivate the majority of parents and their children to involvement in educational attainment in an educational system which, whatever the official intention, rather than demonstrating respect for the individual and the fulfilment of his potential as its ideal, operates to demonstrate and confirm inequality. Stated thus abstractly, this alternative consideration requires elaboration. In the course of discussing the two objectives with which I opened this paper the necessary elaboration will be made.

To turn, then, to my first objective. In this country a powerful stimulus to the furtherance of our understanding of the relationships of environment to attainment was the setting up of the Plowden researches and, more recently, the follow-up studies. Using the findings of the Manchester follow-up study to Plowden in particular I propose to discuss some aspects of the 'traditional wisdom' of environmental researches in this country.

Therefore, if a pupil does not come from a stable home environment, academic failure will be more intrinsic of home environment style

Of the 'findings' from Plowden researches into environment–attainment relationships perhaps the two most generally quoted are:

1 'Home environment is considerably more influential as a determinant of attainment than school.'
2 Of home environmental variables those denoting family attitudes to education, ambition and literacy are a great deal more important than those denoting material circumstances and social class (Wiseman, 1967).

The first finding is, of course, what any thoughtful teacher might have suspected. In essence it is supported by the major analysis carried out in America by Jencks (1972). One response to this finding has been to argue the case for greater involvement of parents in the education of their children. What this might mean in practice could, of course, vary considerably. One suspects that the advocacy of such involvement by individuals and agencies representing quite contrasting ideologies indicates not a common anticipation of the outcome but the likelihood that both elitists and egalitarians see the potential for the furtherance of their own educational and social objectives in the closing of the gap between home and school.[1]

Jencks (1972) takes the argument for parental involvement possibly further than either of the major groups of proponents in this country, and bearing in mind his general ideological stance it is perhaps surprising that he does not realise the potential his proposals have for the

---

[1] At the time of the last Conservative government, for instance, the Education Minister, Mrs Margaret Thatcher, in her concern for the preservation of all kinds of school and parental choice as well of traditional educational methods and 'standards', became a strong advocate of greater parental involvement in what goes on at school. More recently Dr Rhodes Boyson, an MP of similar political persuasion and educational inclination, with characteristic sobriety has in the face of an official administrative conspiracy of silence alerted us all to the violence in secondary schools, the flight of demoralised teachers from our urban areas, the Trotskyite cells of teachers and the professional malcontents seeking, as he sees it, only to destroy our civilisation. The right kind of parents could, of course, become a powerful bulwark against such degenerate influences. (NAS conference, January 1975.) It seems at least likely that those who hold such views will have intentions for parent–teacher contact which differ from those who in a humane and idealistic manner envisage that parents have a right to be closely involved in the formal education of their children and may as a consequence considerably influence the attainments of their children. See, for instance, M. Young and P. McGeeney, *Parents are Welcome*, Routledge, London, 1968.

imposition of conservative ideologies and the entrenchment of elitist control.

The reaction of teachers to proposals for greater parent–teacher involvement, as expressed through their professional bodies, has been highly defensive. To be fair, such relationships do raise difficult questions for the teachers' professional status as widely conceived, and should they ever seriously consider greater parental involvement in schools they would be able to make out a plausible—though not, to my mind, an overwhelming—case for the maintenance of the generally powerful boundaries between themselves and their clients. Such a defence can be made even at a time when research findings have seriously undermined any anticipation that the pursuit of education within the framework of traditional parent–teacher relationships will lead at the primary level to any significant advances in the attainment of educational objectives; and when, as we are currently witnessing, the traditional rationale of secondary education is fast being eroded and the morale of urban secondary teachers is rapidly dwindling.

Before, however, elaborating my discussion of the problems of closer parent–teacher involvement I should like to consider some points arising from the two research findings which, I suggested, were characteristic of environment–attainment analyses at the beginning of this paper. A series of points arise from the frequently made claim that home attitudinal variables are of greater impact upon attainment than those indicating material and socio-economic circumstances. Firstly, and fundamentally, I would like to suggest that there are ideological, empirical and commonsense difficulties in categorising variables in terms of attitudes and material circumstances.

I suggest that within the context of environment–attainment studies as traditionally conducted there can be no empirical justification for categorising some variables as 'attitude variables' and others as circumstance variables. The transposing of a term such as 'attitude', which in some research contexts has a relatively precise though not very useful meaning, to the field of education, where the methods of 'attitude' study are less rigorous and where meanings are less precise, is unjustified empirically and, I would argue, socially irresponsible. In an educational setting such terminology inevitably becomes involved with popular moral and social connotations.

The separation of variables into such categories can be of considerable consequence for the ideological aspects of interpretation and for the determination of policy response. If, for instance, attitudes are regarded as separable from circumstances and, as we have consistently seen (Burt, 1937; Wiseman, 1964, 1967; Peaker, 1971; Bynner, 1971), according to such categorisation are regarded as of more importance for attainment, then certain outcomes become more likely. Firstly, failure to attain is more likely to be attributed to individual waywardness. Secondly, as a likely consequence, the problem of the possible educational threshold effects of variations in the distribution of resources receives less consideration than it should (Byrne et al., 1974).

We cannot justify the separation of environmental variables into 'attitude' and 'circumstance' groupings as though attitudes are formed in the minds of individuals without reference to their circumstances. We know that statements of attitudes may be, and often are, relatively abstracted and idealised; the behavioural outcomes of these statements—which are what really matters so far as the relationship between environment and attainment is concerned—are likely to be significantly mediated by the circumstances in which the process is taking place.

In his researches for the Manchester School of Education and for Plowden the late Stephen Wiseman, who was a major figure in the analysis of the association of environment with attainment in this country, consistently argued the salience of attitudes over circumstance. Acland (1973), commenting on Wiseman's interpretation of his Manchester-based Plowden data writes,

Wiseman's conclusion properly emphasises the literacy of the home as the most important attitudinal comment. This turns out to be the most consistent predictor of achievement, but ... one cannot assume that it represents parents' dispositions. It may equally be a measure of socio-economic status.

In his Plowden follow-up study Peaker tacitly acknowledges the validity of such criticism when he refers to the critics who argued that 'literacy of the home' (1971) was a circumstance rather than an attitude and subsequently transferred the literacy variables in his regression analysis from the attitude composite to that of the parental circumstance composite. The shift is of profound consequence for the traditional view about the relative impact of variable groupings upon attainment. It is clear from Peaker's follow-up analysis that once literacy variables are transferred to material circumstances, then the remaining 'attitudinal' variables are of little consequence for attainment.

In a re-analysis of Peaker's data Acland concludes that 'literacy variables are the most consistent predictor variables . . . The single most important variable is the "whether or not the child is read to" ' (1973).

So far I have made two points relating to the interpretation of attitudes. Firstly I suggested that to talk of attitudes on the basis of inferences drawn from the data collected in the course of environmental analyses of the Plowden type is unsatisfactory. Such inferences are unsatisfactory because they require an unjustifiable degree of ideologically influenced interpretation, which may well in its turn stimulate policies more likely to compound inequalities than to stimulate attempts at their amelioration. Secondly, talk of separating variables into categories of attitudinal and material circumstance encourages the fallacy that they are significantly separable.

I recognise that the first point raises two separate, though to my mind not easily separable, issues. The first relates to the question of objectivity in social science research. The psychometrists who have traditionally dominated environmental research in this country have not seen objectivity as highly problematic. Perhaps because of the abstractions of their mental measurement backgrounds they felt secure in the view that their interpretations of data were highly objective. This is a naive view because essentially their conceptualisation derives from models of men which in themselves have implications for world views or what Gouldner (1971) has called domain assumptions. In other words the models chosen and the interpretations made are determined within the framework of what the individual researcher judges to be plausible on the basis of the fundamental elements which influence his own ideology. The difficulty in the human sciences is that there is never, in the last resort, enough evidence to force us from the global preconceptions which condition our determination of a research problem, the methods by which it may be analysed and the interpretations that we make. If we fail to perceive that even the most abstract models and advanced statistical models when applied to the

human situation secrete, values, then we may have the illusion of objectivity. If, however, we recognise the illusion, then we may be less
complacent, less certain, and the consequence will be that the rigour
of our method will demand value awareness rather than a claim to
value freedom.

It is precisely because of this need for a shift from a claim of objectivity to an attempt at value awareness that I argue my second point,
that is, the essential involvement of the social scientist with a concern
for the policy outcomes of his interpretations. In the past it has often
been argued—partly, I suspect, as a basis of support for the argument
of his objectivity—that the social scientist is not concerned with
policy stemming from his findings. It seems perfectly clear to me that,
given the inevitable subjective element in the social scientist's interpretation, then both as a scientist and as a moral human being he
must emphasise the qualifications to be placed on his findings and the
value basis of his judgements, and that, bearing in mind the relative
nature of values, he must insist that his findings are not used to
justify, or further, prejudice and inequality. I hope it can be
appreciated that I do not regard the points just made as a digression
but see them as fundamental to my whole argument about the dangers
of describing some data as adequate for the inference of attitudes as
separable from circumstances.

In the Manchester follow-up of Plowden which Marjorie Ainsworth
and I (1974) conducted, the association of some indicators of family
literacy often described as attitudinal variables with material circumstances has been consistently evidenced. The clearest example lies in
the association of lack of provision of reading matter with evidence of
poor material circumstances. Another variable, to do with the provision of book storage space for the child, relates more clearly to spatial
considerations, of the child having his own room and of family size,
than to 'attitudes' to literacy.

The intimate association of imputed attitudes with domestic circumstance is again highlighted by the finding that some aspects of
the parents' knowledge of the child's progress—again, variables
described elsewhere in terms of attitudes—are associated with the
mother's occupational circumstance. It was certainly the case for the
Manchester sample that an absence of knowledge about the child's

progress and a lack of educational aspiration were associated with the mother not working and with poor environmental circumstances.

It seems appropriate here to emphasise that those environmental characteristics which have traditionally been described in terms of attitudes to education are also to be seen in the context of the circumstances in which the child is being educated, and that the effect upon attitudes is interactive between the home, the child and the school. Certainly the findings of Bynner (1972) in his Plowden follow-up study seem to support such an interpretation.

If we wish to infer parental educational attitudes from the extent of parental knowledge about school we must have regard to the fact that schools vary greatly in the amount and nature of their communication with the home. It is likely that those schools with the least to offer their charges will communicate least. Since these are the very schools which the most socially disadvantaged and least able children are most likely to attend, research which taps parental knowledge of the child's progress is likely to find that low attainment and low parental knowledge correlate, and may miss the important intervening variables.

Cloward and Jones (1963) suggest that there is unlikely to be a single causal relationship between parents' educational participation and expressed attitudes, and that the more reasonable assumption is that a complicated process of reinforcement and reciprocal causation takes place between 'attitudinal' and circumstance aspects of the environment.

We have not the means of attributing causal priority to one category of variable rather than another, and it has been suggested that parental attitudes to the child's education may be regarded as a consequence of the child's performance in school as well as a cause. I entirely share Acland's view (1973) that 'Since the distinction between attitudes and circumstances is suspect, the statistical analyses which compare their relative effects must be treated with caution'.

Two considerations follow from this discussion of the ways in which environmental variables are categorised for purposes of statistical analysis. Firstly, the fact that we are enabled to make such categorisations is a consequence of the crude analytic process involved; it does not reflect an existing environmental framework. That is, an environment in experience is a total structure, an integrated process of individual meanings made from a complex of gross and subtle interacting influences. Secondly, it is now clear that the terms used to denote variable categories affect the practical and ideological contexts in which interpretations are made.

Thus, for instance, it has sometimes been implied that those who emphasise the role of environment as opposed to the influence of heredity are egalitarians; alternatively those who argue in favour of inherited determinates of ability are sometimes described as elitists. Certainly in the present discussion of attitudes and circumstances it has tended to be the sociologists who have argued against separation into such categories, and neither Burt (1955) nor Wiseman (1964) was reticent in the view that sociologists are motivated by egalitarian, if not more sinister, ideologies.

So far as practical contexts are concerned it becomes somewhat more likely that if literacy variables become interpreted as circumstances, then they may be regarded as somehow being more the consequence of social influences and more potentially amenable to social action. If, on the other hand, literacy variables are seen as attitudes, they may be seen as representing in those with 'poor' attitudes (i.e. low scores) recalcitrance, indifference and sometimes even inability. Clearly there are striking differences to be anticipated in the response to be made, according to the categorisation involved.

There are two further matters relating to problems of environmental analysis which are evidenced by the findings of the Manchester Plowden follow-up. These relate to the tendency to assume that the effect of an environmental influence is constant across social classes and through time.

The Manchester survey provides some evidence to suggest that there may be some differentiation in the impact of maternally rooted variables through time. It appears likely that the influence of the father as an educational strategist, as an occupational role model and as a determinant of material circumstances becomes increasingly influential as the child grows older. The mother's more diffuse supportive role becomes relatively less important.

For the highest levels of attainment, of course, the child's own aspirations come into close association with those of the parents, although here again it must be emphasised that analysis also indicates the considerable importance of school setting in association with high levels of aspiration.

At an early stage of this discussion it was suggested that the relative unimportance of material circumstance compared with attitudes was a fairly consistent finding of environmental analysts. In the Manchester survey it is clear that as education proceeds so material circumstance variables gain in importance, having their major impact upon attainment at sixteen-plus (Batten, 1974). Staying on for one extra year and sixteen-plus attainment are associated overwhelmingly with favourable environmental circumstances, and staying on seems to be a better predictor of secondary performance at this level than attainment at ten-plus.

Sixteen-plus attainment and seventeen-plus attainment are relatively independent of ability measured at ten-plus. For the child who leaves at fifteen correlations with both attainment and environmental varibles are consistently negative from seven-plus onwards. Poor environmental conditions are clearly associated with statutory leavers.

The sixth-form entrant is environmentally distinguished from the sixteen-plus leaver by better housing circumstances and by a mother who is not working. In this case 'mother not working' is an indication of a favourable environment, whereas for the statutory leaver 'mother not working' has unfavourable environmental associations. Other environmental variables also indicate the middle-classness of sixth-form entrants and, of course, the importance of school context.

We cannot suggest that if statutory leavers stayed on at secondary school they would attain well; the primary school attainments of statutory leavers in our survey were generally poor. What is clear, however, is that the motivation to stay on is strongly associated with good material circumstances and a favourable school environment. It appears from the Manchester survey that those aspects of the environment determining the decision to leave school at the earliest possible moment are already apparent by the time of entry to secondary school. The will to attain, as evidenced by staying on at school, is seen as having quite an important effect in an educatively supportive environment. Whilst recognising the relative incapacity of schools to affect significantly either the home environment or the pattern of opportunities in the wider society for the majority of pupils, it seems legitimate to speculate upon whether the education system could not, if it were so desired, become more internally supportive, and more effective in nourishing the desire to attain.

The importance of school setting requires emphasis. It seems at least doubtful whether an educational system which has the effect of systematically selecting the most advantaged members of the school population for further advantage can effectively motivate those not so selected to want education.

It is suggested, then, that parental influence and material circumstances may vary in their impact upon attainment through time and that school setting may be highly influential in its impact. Material circumstances, though traditionally regarded as of little consequence, appear to be highly influential in their effect upon the leaving decision.

Undoubtedly the clearest predictor of attainment at secondary school, even after controlling for ability at entry, is a place in a selective setting. The analysis of school environments in the Plowden follow-up for Manchester provided clear evidence of the superior educational facilities as well as the environmental advantages of the selective intake. Perhaps it is the selective schools which most value and support those aspects of the home environment associated with attainment, literacy and ambition. For such schools ambition is appropriate. They can confirm future social and economic advantage to a significant proportion of their population. For those who value literacy ambition need not be a highly conscious process; the educational system is such that those in selective schools can, if they wish—especially on the arts side—keep their options open and drift upwards through the educational system without very precise occupational goals in view. Although in the selective setting with a high chance of future success it is possible to emphasise the pursuit of education for its intrinsic worth and deny instrumental involvement, there is no doubt that the pursuit of literacy is closely associated with future opportunity through the traditional external examination system. This happy coincidence is denied to the non-selected and lower-stream child, for whom both the intrinsic satisfactions and extrinsic rewards of education are extremely limited.

However, before developing a discussion of the various proposals

which have been made for the amelioration of the educational circumstances and attainments of the disadvantaged I want to discuss a
related question that we asked ourselves when interpreting the data of
the Manchester follow-up. We were concerned to uncover those
aspects of environmental influene which might be regarded as most
amenable to external influence.

When the average secondary attainment–environment correlations
were partialled for the effects of parental ability, indicated by parents'
claimed eleven-plus success, and for the effects of child's ability on
the basis of ability as indicated at seven-plus it was evident that the
parents' ability has a lesser impact upon attainment–environment correlations than that of the child. It is suggested, however, that in practice it is parents who have the major capacity for influencing many
aspects of the home environment, especially in areas usually described
as attitudinal and in the area of material circumstance. The
Manchester survey indicated that several variables characterised as in-
dicative of attitudes to education and literacy are relatively independent of parental ability, and it is argued that they are in principle those
aspects of environment most amenable to the influence of external
agencies, such as libraries and schools.

The parents of secondary school children have seldom been the
subjects of systematic attempts to enroll their support in the pursuit of
better attainment by their children. The analysis of the schools side of
the Manchester follow-up survey provides strong support for this
view.

The home environment analysis powerfully suggests the extent to
which schools control the information made available to parents; are
influential in the development of the child's and the parents' ambition;
can influence supportiveness with homework, and play an influential
role in an elaborate process of interaction between parents, child and
school.

It has traditionally been suggested that parental attitudes to education may be the more important environmental influences upon the attainments of the child. At the secondary stage the child's attitudes to
education are undoubtedly important too, and it may well be that
future environmental researches could usefully concern themselves
with the gross and subtle institutional and organisational influences

which impinge upon the child's attitudinal development.

Until we are a great deal more knowledgeable about how people learn, how to teach them effectively, and the nature of the influence of environmental characteristics upon their motivation we cannot hope to assess the limits of individual potential. Nor indeed can we accept the present indications as providing strong evidence that we have so far measured the impact of the school upon attainment.

It appears that within the limitations of current modes of analysis we find that individual school environmental variables are of little or inconsistent consequence for attainment. We also find evidence for the view that there are considerable disparities in the provision of educational resources within and between schools, the commonest characteristic of this disparity being that those pupils least well endowed environmentally and intellectually get the poorest school resources.

If this state of affairs were the consequence of a conscious educational policy it would be seen as paradoxical in the extreme. Certainly it would be a consequence without parallel if it really was the case that to deny the pupil the stimulation of adequate resources and conditions is the most effective way of promoting educational attainment, the development of a healthy self-image and high ambition. The more equitable distribution of resources might well be of consequence for the development of school environments in which educationally helpful orientations could develop and in which educational attainments might improve.

Nevertheless, to return to the level of home environmental influence, it is suggested from the Manchester research that parents' involvement with the education of their children is relatively independent of parental ability. Even in that area of environmental analysis where parental ability seems to have the greatest consequence the variables involved frequently relate to parents' educational knowledge or factual information. These are in principle amenable to attempts not previously made to influence or inform the parents.

Perhaps the underlying problem in terms of schools developing more effective means of communication and systematic methods of influencing attitudes is one which cannot be dealt with simply. It is suggested that with their occupational orientation secondary schools have no plausible case which they could employ to involve the majority of parents to motivate their offspring to higher levels of attainment.

In some educational settings educational ambitions are unrealistic, and it is in the context of the educational setting that educational attitudes may be most objectively interpreted. It may be that some parents hold attitudes to school and education (and these are not always synonymous) which are not useful; but then, if education is not, for them or their offspring, functional it is not easy to appreciate why we should expect them to value it. It is unsatisfactory to interpret their attitudes as existing in a vacuum, as if to imply that those attitudes would necessarily be the same if their objective circumstances changed.

It appears that what we infer as attitudes from statements of hopes, intentions and expectations are to some extent separable from both parental and child abilities. To that extent it may be possible for the school and other agencies to guide parents in their highly influential role of affecting the child's educational attainment.

Parents' ignorance of the child's attainments is not always associated with indifference to the child and his performance but must be seen in the context of the school's having considerable freedom in determining the information which it provides for parents and the amount of contact they have with it.

Similarly, attitudes to literacy are not entirely determined by the ability level of parents or child. The *amount* of parents' reading is less dependent than the *level* of parents' reading upon their ability and more associated with the child's school attainment. If literacy is important for attainment it is easy to see that library provision is likely to be an important agency in its furtherance. The implementation of a useful attitude to literacy seems often associated with material circumstances, and the provision of free reading material through a convenient local source may help in situations where economic circumstances are unfavourable.

Perhaps arising from the previous considerations we might suggest that not only are educational attitudes formed on the basis of interaction between parent, child, school and teachers but also with reference to material aspects of the environment. Just as parents' ambition and expectation develop through their interpretation of the capacities, ambitions and expectations of the child and his teachers in the light of their previous experiences, so their planning and educational strategies, their discussions and their detailed considerations are conducted with reference to the realities indicated to them by their present circumstances. Thus we find, for instance, that detailed knowledge of the child's progress in individual subjects is associated not only with variables suggesting a selective school setting but also with variables related to the size of the family and adequate space in the home.

The educational attitudes developed by parents are for the most part realistic; useful educational attitudes associate more with a selective setting, good school support and good material circumstances. A low valuation of education is more associated with non-selective settings, poor school support and poor material circumstances. It is not clear how we might effectively change the 'attitudes' of those who are thus disadvantaged.

The education system has minimal scope for advantageously influencing the social and economic experiences of the considerable majority of the school population, yet at the same time schools cling to structures and practices which reflect the traditional functionalist viewpoint of the role of education. The functionalist view leads not simply to the creation of educational structures for the selection of a minority for economic and social promotion; it involves, for the majority, a process of negative selection, a confirmation of the disadvantages that the child brings with him to school.

It may, of course, be argued that parents, teachers and pupils do not view education from a sociologically sceptical standpoint, that the assumptions of the role of education are not questioned. I suggest that teachers (themselves streamed) in non-selective schools and in the lower streams of comprehensive schools are likely to have a very clear idea of the motivational inadequacy of the claim that working hard at school will bring future advantage. They will have gained these perceptions through their own professional socialisation; through their observation of the disparity in the distribution of educational resources and through their knowledge of where education leads for the majority of their charges.

In the Manchester sub-sample study the analysis revealed a strong association between a selective setting and attainment in all subjects. It seems likely that the attitudes of parents and schools to literacy and attainment usually match, and that as far as the progress of the child at school is concerned we are witnessing a reciprocal and reinforcing process.

Secondary education, with its highly instrumental associations, is likely, through the way in which it structures the pattern of future opportunity, to create appropriately depressed school settings as well as appropriately ambitious school settings. In socially and educationally depressed settings neither appeals to ambition nor appeals to intrinsic educational satisfactions can be expected to motivate good attainment.

The fact that many families already opt out of anything but a minimal involvement in education, combined with the accumulating academic evidence of the great distance between education's objectives and its practical outcome, must create increasing pressure for a more widely based discussion of the assumptions upon which our education system is based. If teachers and educationists are to bring about such a dialectic through closer relations between home and school, then the dilemma which is facing them is clear: the activities in which parents and teachers become involved might well be more political than educational. It is particularly with this problem that I come to the final section of my paper.

If inequality of opportunity for education began at home and was separable from the wider inequalities of our society, then it might be reasonable to anticipate that ameliorative policies within schools and communities could change the patterns of motivation for educational attainment. The fact is, however, that in a society in which equality of opportunity is a widely acknowledged social and educational objective, inequality is an entrenched and inherent part of our social organisation. The concepts of equality and of average ability—both of considerable currency within education—carry with them an implicit denial of the uniqueness of individuals, and by a process of intellectual elision make it likely that those who are less than equal in their access to social resources and less than average in terms of performance on educational test scores or their placement in the educational system come to be regarded as less than average or less than equal people (Newsom, 1963). The disvaluing mechanisms of social and educational selection deriving from our willingness to categorise individuals according to arbitrarily defined and, in the case of education, irrelevant criteria are the key to the mechanisms both gross and subtle which result in the inequitable distribution of resources. There is an apparent irony in the fact that the very arbitrary, conditional and abstracted categories employed for the definition of problems by social scientists become reified by governments as a basis for action, and in becoming so are further instruments for discrimination and prejudice.

Our society offers highly predictable sets of life chances. Clearly some individuals are motivated to beat the predictions, and do so. Most do not, otherwise actuarial assessments would not hold up. Most have a pretty clear understanding of what their social expectations are. The same is true in education. The considerable array of information (of varying degrees of subtlety) that parents and their children receive combine to encourage a fairly unambiguous set of predictions concerning a child's educational and social future. Within education itself the evidence of inter- and intra-regional variations in educational support (Byrne and Williamson, 1972) and organisation (Taylor and Ayres, 1969) is quite clear and generally in accord with the relationship that those who start life with the highest indices of disadvantage receive the resources offering the narrowest range of opportunity.

The call for positive discrimination is one response to this phenomenon, and represents a recognition of the concept of equity rather than of equality as being the more relevant in the ordering of human affairs, and particularly of education. Even so, administrative expediency requires that in the first instance such discrimination should be group-based rather than individually oriented. At the secondary level the major response, so far, to combat the inequitable effects of selection and categorisation procedures has been to encourage the development of comprehensive education. Whilst I am unequivocally in favour of comprehensive education, on educational grounds, there is no reason to assume that its introduction will in the short or even medium term significantly ameliorate the inequity of the wider society. Further, comprehensive developments so far have overwhelmingly maintained the selection and grouping devices of the old tripartite system. The barriers which existed before have been subsumed under the roof of a single institution: there are still the significant sorting points within compulsory education (Benn and Simon, 1970); there are still the clearest indications in the organisational characteristics of the overwhelming majority of schools of their anticipation of the child's educational performance and of his future social destination. Further, of course, there remain many schools which continue to service a privileged minority and which by their apparent success in securing the future advantage of their pupils exercise an undue influence on the characteristics of secondary schools in the State system. The comprehensive school is very likely to become the area school, attracting resources according to the educational status of its staff and the social class background of its area.

One response to a growing awareness of this likelihood has been the development of a call for community schools. It is not immediately apparent how such developments can change the general position which has already been elaborated. To be fair, this has already been argued by Halsey (1972), and the moral point is accepted, that the raising of educational standards—especially of the most disadvantaged—should be undertaken for its own sake. Whatever our researches have shown concerning the lack of consistent association of school environmental variables with attainment, it certainly seems unlikely that we might expect that those with the least material resources and indicating the least measured abilities will improve in their attainments if we give them the least satisfactory educational support, which is, on the whole, what happens now.

It has been repeatedly suggested that parents' attitudes to education are more important than their material circumstances. It has seemed to follow, therefore, that by changing the nature of their involvement with parents schools might harness parental influence for the purpose of improving the child's attainments. I have previously argued that the separation of variables into those of circumstance and attitude represents a serious over-simplification, and that family dispositions to education do not develop in a vacuum but are the consequence of a total interactive process. I would like to suggest that not only are the parents' ambitions for their children usually rooted in their objective situation and some sense of their child's capacities, but that so also are the attitudes of teachers which have led to the present patterns of association between home and school. In other words, certainly by the secondary stage it is difficult to see just what schools can communicate to parents which could change their perceptions in the face of their wider experience and accumulated judgements concerning the role of education in affecting their child's future opportunity. This is, of course, true for the majority of the school population. Clearly the intervention of teachers in individual situations can be highly influential. Advantage is by definition limited and relative, and it is not possible to anticipate that the implementation of a general programme of close parent–teacher contact could significantly affect overall patterns of motivation to attain within the context of an instrumentally oriented education system. Teachers probably recognise also that within the confines of polite professional conversation they have little more to communicate to parents than the oracular comments, sometimes constructive, that appear on report forms once or twice a year.

The closer association of parents and teachers, even supposing it can be brought about, must be regarded as a very dubious enterprise if the role of the teacher in these circumstances is seen as that of a troubleshooter for the inadequacies of the educational system and the inequalities of the wider society—if he is encouraged to act in such a way as to persuade parents that the highly bureaucratised system of occupational selection which now passes for secondary education in our society is something they should cheerfully accept, and that they should conspire in the maintenance of an educational system which serves principally to confirm the social disadvantages with which they have endowed their offspring.

Alternatively teachers might become involved with parents, dare I say it, politically. There is an irony here. Is it any less political for teachers to continue to conceal from parents their function of educating for the confirmation of incompetence (Turner, 1961) and disadvantage or to seek to reconcile them to the maldistribution of educational resources than it is to attempt to indicate to them their power as agents with influence, if they wish to exert it, over the ways in which educational and social resources are distributed? I believe not (indeed, I believe that we delude ourselves if we do not appreciate that in many respects education is a political activity), though I do not for a moment anticipate that anything like a majority of teachers would agree with me.

It seems clear that there are, then, considerable difficulties relating to a definition of professional integrity involved in closer teacher–parent relationships. Quite apart from such professional difficulties, however, the growing evidence of the lack of impact of education upon the distribution of life chances; the absence of certainty concerning the effectiveness of pedagogical skills; the implausibility of the defence of education for its own sake; and last, though possibly not least, the lack of popular respectability of teachers' academic knowledge, especially sociology; all serve to make me doubtful whether the teaching profession will indulge in any significant extension of its relationship with the outside world, especially at the secondary level. It is too insecure in itself to undertake any major involvement in an exercise in its own demystification. It has a vested interest in the examinations industry and the status hierarchies which go with it. The existing system is that in which teachers have mostly been socialised, it has played an important part in helping the teacher to gain his professional identity and has quite likely been the basis on his own upward social mobility.

Quite apart for being reasons why I doubt whether any significant increase in parent–teacher contact will take place, they also amount to a basis for doubting whether community schools, with their essentially unbureaucratic approach to education, local teacher–parent-defined goals, community-based curricula, and local involvement, with a high political potential and locally designed organisational characteristics, will find extensive professional support from teachers—or, indeed, administrative and political support—once the full implications are recognised. Proposals for community schools contain within them too great a potential for quite basic questions to be asked about educational and social objectives.

A central difficulty with community schools at the secondary level is determining where they might fit into the existing educational system. If they are to become in effect a category of schools for the disadvantaged, then although they may be better and happier social institutions for those involved in them, and they may lead to higher levels of attainment than might otherwise have been attained, they cannot anticipate that by substituting an ecological curriculum for the traditional academic one they will do more than intensify a sense of educational *apartheid* and seriously exacerbate the question of the political involvement of teachers. For such schools to become the standard they would need espousing by the middle class, who have, at least up to now, exercised the greatest power and influence in the distribution of social resources, largely to their own advantage. Within the present educational ethos, community schools are unlikely to appeal to more than an eccentric fringe of the middle class whose educational idealism has served to blind it to the risk that by accepting such schools it may be missing a chance to provide its children with the smoothest possible path to the confirmation of their future social status.

If community schools accept the characteristics of the wider system and at the secondary level attempt to integrate through their involvement in external examinations, it is again not easy to see how they can avoid contamination by those educational values which have served within the existing educational framework to demotivate the disadvantaged for attainment. Essentially these are the values which emphasise the unequalness of individuals rather than their uniqueness. They invoke selection and competition; they emphasise ascribed status relationships and hierarchy; they define attainment narrowly in terms of academic excellence rather than in terms of excellence, academic excellence being assessed by external examinations which seldom, if ever, may be regarded as indicating academic attainment or a level of excellence in any educational sense.

What, then, are the solutions to the dilemmas which I have tried to outline? It would be to ignore the evidence which informs my judgement, against the spirit of what I have tried to say here and of what I believe in, to proffer the dogmas of simple solutions. One thing is, however, clear. The present state of our knowledge no longer allows the comfortable assumption that education is a significant agent in reducing social inequity.

If we wish to preserve the characteristics of the existing system, which, historically, developed piecemeal and has only subsequently had a supposedly coherent 'explanation' of its role imposed upon it, then we are bound to discover a new rationale for continuing with an educational system the organisational characteristics of which are, as we may observe, educationally dysfunctional for the majority and socially and economically irrelevant overall—at least in terms of the acceptable objectives of an educational system in a democratic society. This appears to me to be an impossible task, and yet I suppose it fair to suggest that an education which has the capacity to absorb considerable resources, most of which are provided by those who receive least (Glennerster, 1972), should have a rationale—a series of coherently stated objectives which provide the basis for a critical assessment of procedures.

My own view is that the evidence now to hand provides the basis of a powerful argument for freeing education from the bureaucratic entanglement which has occurred in the cause of equality of opportunity and the assumption of its social and economic expedience; that we should perhaps seek the more personal, local and relevant forms of education during the compulsory stages, which is what, I take it, community-based education implies. We should do this through following up in practical terms the implications of the concepts of equity and individuality in education and through the assumption of a client-centred consumption ethos rather than the current system-centred investment models of education. The difficulties have not been under-estimated, and without the application of the community concept as a national policy there can be little hope of success. We need, however, to emphasise that, whilst community-based education may have as its intention the better attainments of individuals through their initial stimulation by a sense of education's relevance, we are seeking also to develop the capacity for universality. An education which aids the rejection of 'community' boundaries, boundaries which in the long run can be maintained only by prejudice. This is important, because the local community organisation has at least as high a potential for tyrannising individuals and denying their individuality as any central government agency. So far as education is concerned, the individual may be as much threatened by the parochialism of a curriculum as by a depersonalised educational system in which organisation becomes an end in itself.

The advantage—the overwhelming advantage—of a community school system is that it could operate a form of education completely divorced from considerations of selection and the instrumental connotations of the existing system. It would have the potential at least for emphasising through an individualistic approach the affective satisfactions of education. Through the shared involvement in a local and socially oriented curriculum the teacher may evince a level of concern, interest and acknowledgement of the validity of the community experience which can influence parent–pupil acceptance of his affective valuation of education. None of these outcomes is inevitable, but unless they are intended there appears to be no significant educational reason to argue for a change to the community school concept.

Nevertheless if the analysis that I have made is accepted, then it is difficult to see how the informed teacher can feel confident in asserting the validity of the present system or hopeful of any substantial change for the better in the educational outcome as a result of minor modifications.

4

A. H. HALSEY *Educational Priority Areas*

The Oxford study of educational priority areas was an action research project in four EPAs (Deptford, in London; Balsall Heath, in Birmingham; Liverpool 8; and Denaby Main, in the West Riding). There was a fifth, parallel Scottish study in Dundee. A general conspectus of our findings appeared as volume 1 of a five-volume series in 1972. The other four volumes appeared in 1974.

My purpose in this paper is to summarise the project as a whole, to point to subsequent developments and to reassert the potential contribution of the EPA idea to the raising of educational standards, especially among those who are described by the modern euphemism as 'the disadvantaged'.

Our major conclusions from the four English EPA action research projects were that:

1 The educational priority area, despite its difficulties of definition, is a socially and administratively viable unit through which to apply the principle of positive discrimination.
2 Pre-schooling is the oustandingly economical and effective device in the general approach to raising educational standards in EPAs.
3 The idea of the community school, as put forward in skeletal outline by Plowden, has now been shown to have greater substance and powerful implications for community regeneration.
4 There are practical ways of improving the partnership between families and schools in EPAs.
5 There are practical ways of improving the quality of teaching in EPA schools.

6   Action research is an effective method of policy formation and practical innovation.

7   The EPA can be no more than a part, though an important one, of a comprehensive social movement towards community development and community redevelopment in a modern urban industrial society.

Defining educational priority areas

Good ideas for social policy often founder through maladroit translation into administrative practice. The essential idea of EPA is to produce a quantitative measure of concentration in a given area of the social 'have-nots' and to turn this assessment of disadvantage into a financial formula of positive discrimination which would determine the flow of extra resources from central to local government for education. The ILEA index is widely acknowledged to be the most sophisticated attempt at definition so far. More work needs to be done to produce a designation of areas of special concern by objective, reproducible criteria. But there can be no national and mechanical. solution. There is no rational answer to the problem of weighting the different factors such as unemployment, bad housing, child poverty or teacher turnover which indicate social disadvantage and which have to be translated into an administrative definition. Moreover no system of weighting is likely to be satisfactory for every local area in the country. There is not just one kind of EPA constellation of conditions. And there must therefore be room for local adaptation according to local needs.

Thus the typical EPA is situated in the inner ring of a conurbation where social stress through overcrowding and multi-occupation is rife and there are often particular problems of language and schooling associated with immigration. On the other hand, these areas are, on the whole, ones of high employment. The West Riding project revealed that there are other kinds of EPA area. In this case the outstanding feature was that of poor economic prospects. Denaby Main is an example of the collapse and decay of a small town based on a single industry. It did not suffer, as the EPA schools in conurbations typically do, from high turnover of either teachers or pupils at a rate which makes the running of a school a difficult if not impossible exercise.

But quite apart from these problems of variations in conditions (which bedevil the task of constructing a map of EPA conditions in such a way as to administer the distribution of funds in relation to educational poverty) there is an even more difficult problem. This is the difficulty that, however the map is drawn, it is bound to include some non-EPA children and exclude others who have the disadvantages which are concentrated in but not exclusive to the EPA district. No one, presumably, has ever supposed that all social deprivation with educational consequences can be delineated on a map. Nor does anyone suppose that all the worst schools are concentrated in EPAs nor all the pupils of lowest attainment in the schools identified as EPA. In volume 3 Jack Barnes has emphasised this point and has produced some arithmetic of the degree to which the mapping approach diverges from the actual distribution of disadvantaged individuals. Clearly, then, positive discrimination on an area basis can never be a complete policy. It has to be complemented by individual diagnosis and care in the education and social services. Nevertheless we did not reject the notion of educational priority *areas* as distinct from schools or individuals. On the contrary, we would still argue that the locality focus is essential to the general character of a policy for community schooling.

Pre-schooling

Pre-schooling played a crucial part in our EPA action research programme. There was an attempt at a national experiment to test the utility of an element of structured learning in pre-school programmes which is reported in detail by Joan Payne in volume 2. There was also a series of innovations of varying character in each of the four English EPA districts.

Our first and major conclusion from pre-schooling experience is that this holds out promise of a foundation for the development of community schooling. It is the point at which, properly understood, the networks of family and formal education can most easily be linked. It is the point at which the traditional barriers between the influences of school and community can most easily be broken. It is the point where a new teaching professionalism, seeing itself as supportive to the educative influence of the family, can most appropriately begin.

We concluded, second, that pre-schooling is an apt instrument for applying the principle of positive discrimination. In this respect I would lay particular emphasis on one of the West Riding in-novations—the home visitor—which has been spreading rapidly through the country ever since. In thinking about this idea I drew an analogy with the earlier experience of the health visiting service. That service was a positive discriminatory response to a situation in which the national culture of 'post-germ theory' care for young children needed to be spread to the whole population, partly on the grounds of the right of all individuals to take advantage of advances in the culture of their society and partly to make maximally effective the improve-ment of life chances which had come about through sanitary, dietary and medical progress. Though it preceded the invention of the label, the health visiting service was a notable example of positive dis-crimination. The health visitor distributed energies according to a detailed local knowledge of the incidence of need. Life chances today seem to me to depend much more than ever before on the capacity of families to bring up their children with the skill and motivation to use the resources of opportunities offered by the educational system. These skills and resources are unevenly distributed socially and need to be incorporated into the life of every family. The educational health visitor can therefore be an agent of positive discrimination at the pre-school level and simultaneously is, in effect, working also in the field of adult education.

Our EPA experience also taught us that there is no unique blueprint of either organisational content which can be standardised as national policy. Indeed, it is absolutely essential to develop a sensitive educational anthropology so as to diagnose the needs of individual children and of particular EPA districts to produce a flexible provi-sion of nursery education for children under five. Certainly we were not recommending a national provision for the reduction of the school starting age to four years and certainly we did not want to encourage the government to ignore the past labours and potential energies of the voluntary movements in this field. One of the most encouraging and impressive aspects of the development of voluntary movements like the Birmingham PPA is that they enliven the community life of particular localities, primarily by involving mothers in pre-school activities but secondarily and consequentially in a larger network of social relationships which make for an improved quality of life in ways which no bureaucratically organised public service could ever achieve.

These pre-school movements have relevance for all classes of society and for social life generally as well as for educational experience in particular. But, of course, the thrust of our own interest was to recommend that, in so far as limited governmental funds were concerned, the available resources should be concentrated for the most part in the EPA districts.

As to organisation, then, we advocated the idea of the nursery centre which would be neither the expensive professionally run nursery school nor the cheap and parent-run amateur play group. Behind this general proposal lay, on the one hand, our insistence that the home is the most important educational influence on the child and, on the other, our conception of the appropriate role of professional pedagogy in a modern society.

On this latter point we have to recognise that there are two contrasting traditions of pre-schooling: the nursery class and the play group. The first and official tradition has the disadvantages of high cost and a professional orientation which on the whole discourages parental involvement. At the same time it has the tremendous advantage of high standards. Play groups, on the other hand, have reciprocal qualities: they are cheap, typically ill equipped in inadequate premises, but they do encourage co-operation from parents. Our hybrid organisational proposal is an attempt to encourage the fusion of these two traditions on the basis of what I have described as local educational anthropology in determining the needs of each particular district.

We hoped that at the Whitehall level a new division would emerge, presumably based in the DES but with close links with the relevant functions of the DHSS and the Home Office, having responsibility for pre-schooling and with special responsibility for educational priority areas.

At the local level we looked for partnership between statutory and voluntary effort. What was needed, we thought, was a co-ordinated format of pre-school provision, under the guidance and help of local authority advisers, and including a variety—in style, location and time—of play groups grouped around the LEA nursery schools, classes and primary schools and also the day nurseries. Our experimental districts had provided numerous illustrations of possible variations in this type of organisation, adapted to the needs of localities. Eric Midwinter has elaborated his approach to these problems in Liverpool. Volume 4, on the West Riding, includes an account of the home visiting programme and of pre-school activity at the now famous Red House.

The Red House originated in Sir Alec Clegg's call for the setting up of hostels to provide short-term residential care for schoolchildren during periods of crisis in the home. It was not, as such, a scheme confined to pre-schooling but was developed by the action research team to include a range of community education services. Red House became a multi-purpose centre serving as an adjunct to schools in the immediate area and including pre-school work. In the course of a year it was estimated that about a thousand different children had been involved at the centre for various lengths of time. The house was used throughout the day and in the evenings by many small groups. Children of pre-school, infant, junior and secondary age were involved, as well as parents, teachers and other members of the community. Students from local teacher training colleges worked there, and a number of people in the social services departments used it as a contact point for the area. In the evenings parent groups came together for sessions such as cookery demonstrations, and at times for meetings with teachers about education.

Thus the Red House could be seen as incorporating a possible form of the nursery centre we advocated. There was strong parental involvement in the afternoon nursery groups. As children approached school entry, preliminary reading work was introduced. Experiments were made with individual language work. The parents were involved and enthusiastic. The teacher in charge also made home visits, and from this a parents' group developed, with regular meetings in the evenings. Children from the secondary schools also participated, and this had a remarkable effect on some girls and boys enduring, as they tended to see it, the last year before being released from school to life. The Red House Education Centre, in short, successfully and dramatically illustrates how pre-schooling can be incorporated into a community organisation formed by co-operation between statutory and voluntary bodies. It suits the local character of a relatively isolated mining town and it continues on its successful way.

The community school

Though pre-schooling was the first major theme of the EPA project, and the one to which there could be a direct governmental response, there was another and no less important side to our activities—the community school. The idea of the community school had appeared in an elementary form in the Plowden report. As a result of EPA experience I am convinced that the general principle of the community school is the most radically progressive element for the future development of education to emerge in the past few years. A pre-school programme of the kind we have advocated (informed, that is, by the working principles of parental co-operation, statutory and voluntary association, local diagnosis of need and positive discrimination) fits into the foundations of the concept of the community school. This type of schooling in turn is congruent with the even broader idea of recurrent education which constitutes a programme for the realisation of 'the learning society'.

This is not to say, however, that especially after our EPA experience, we have retained the naive utopianism which can so easily give meaning or meaninglessness to community. Indeed, I thoroughly agree with the attitude expressed by Basil Bernstein (1969) towards rudimentary conceptions of the community school as 'merely a new name for play centres, youth clubs and evening institutes, with lip service to Henry Morris, meeting in school premises'. But when the idea is taken seriously, i.e. when it is based on full recognition of the fact that learning, whether positive or negative, is a dimension of all social relationships into which the individual enters at any point in his lifetime, new directions and potentials of collaboration between school, home and the wider social environment come into view.

Let me argue the case by considering what is perhaps a caricature of our traditional concept of the school. A school, it may be said, is a place where teachers teach children. This banality may be represented as in fig. 4.1. The arrow, of course, represents the transmission of knowledge and may have a positive or negative value.

FIG. 4.1.

But we also know that parents teach children, and indeed the major critique of schooling over the past generation has been along the lines of emphasising that the family in its context of class, status, power and ethnicity is the *major* educative force in the life of any child. We may therefore amend the diagram to transform it into a triangle in which *P* may serve simplistically to represent the learning dimension of the relationship of a child to his parents, to peers and other persons in the community to which he belongs inside as well as outside school. The diagram therefore becomes as fig. 4.2.

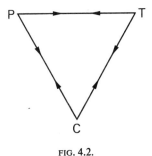

FIG. 4.2.

In this way we are led to substitute for the single vector a triangle in which arrows of the transmission of knowledge run both ways on each of the three sides. Of course teachers teach children, but so do parents, and to this we must now add that children can teach teachers and parents as well as that teachers can teach parents and parents can teach teachers. The essential general point is that this elaboration of the traditional stereotype of learning has brought us to a definition of the community school. The community school can be said to exist in a serious way when each of the six arrows on the three sides of the triangle has a positive value. I believe that we have here a convenient way of analysing the strengths and deficiencies of existing schooling at all levels and for non-EPA as well as EPA conditions. Perhaps I may illustrate the point by some further remarks about the profession of teaching.

Cultural transmission began to be professionalised in the nineteenth century with the emergence of differentiated cadres of trained teachers. The modernisation of societies through the development of industrial techniques and the emergence of predominantly urban patterns of life produced conditions which, in effect, specialised the family and generated a large range of other specialised institutions in the economy and the realms of government, religion and leisure through which the individual attains a more or less satisfactory and advantageous connection to life chances. From one point of view the upbringing of children in the period of modernisation has become a shifting balance between the older 'amateur' forces of family and kinship and the newer, characteristically bureaucratised 'professional' forces of teaching, medicine, social work and public administration.

Where disadvantage to the child appears there is always a case for displacement of the amateur by the professional. The dilemma runs deep in our society as between a commitment to the obvious advantages of upbringing in families and the different but no less real advantages offered by professional child care in all its forms. This dilemma expresses itself with particular poignancy in the case of children who grow up under the worst conditions of social disadvantage. The dilemma is, then, one between displacement of the amateur and support for him or her. On the whole, the traditions in professional education have been those of displacement. But the idea of the community school is one which embodies a movement towards support rather than displacement. It involves a more difficult and sophisticated professionalism than does the alternative principle. But if that set of professional skills and organisational flexibility can be developed, then the learning process for children—and indeed for people at any age or stage—can be immeasurably improved.

The rudiments of community schooling are well known. What I am advocating, however, is a full development of the linkage of school to family, school to teacher training, school to economy and school to school which is implied by the community school idea. It is not to be dismissed as an impracticable approach. Quite apart from our EPA experience, it is encouraging to hear of the spread of ambitious community schooling ideas in many parts of England and Wales. For example, I would cite the remarkably successful experiment of formal incorporation of parents into the life of primary schools in Dorset which Mr A. J. Wood reported in his doctoral thesis at the University of Southampton this year.

Conclusion

The problem in education, as we all know, is not so much to innovate as to consolidate. When a major action research programme like EPA is completed it becomes urgent to disseminate the findings, including the failures as well as the successes. A good deal of dissemination of EPA ideas has taken place through conferences, lectures, new teaching in colleges of education and especially through the energetic activities of Eric Midwinter in Priority and ACE. How far the ideas of pre-schooling and community schooling have been original to the EPA project and how far stimulated by them only the future social historian will be able to determine. I must say, however, that I have been disappointed that the DES has not taken a more direct role in the dissemination process,[1] though I have considerable respect for the efforts made by HMIs and others to play this role as part of their ordinary duties.

There was, of course, a direct response from the Conservative ad-

---

[1] There has now been some governmental action on this front. Mr Prentice, while Secretary of State for Education, set up both a unit inside the DES and a centre to operate from Manchester under the chairmanship of Sir Alec Clegg. These two bodies, especially the latter, should improve the dissemination process.

ministration to which we reported our findings and recommendations, though the action research programme had been commissioned by the previous administration. A White Paper, *Framework for Expansion*, appeared late in 1972 and heralded Margaret Thatcher's determination to make a significant mark on the British educational system during her term of office as Secretary of State. I wrote an immediate response to the White Paper in *The Times Educational Supplement* which I would like to repeat without apology for the lack of solemnity in its style.

Mrs Thatcher's White Paper

Governments sometimes behave like travel agents. They use White Papers to attract us to future excursions. Mrs Thatcher's brochure is the first full catalogue to be issued since 1944. Some old resorts, like the comprehensive school, have been dropped. There are also vast territories in *l'education permanente* which remain uncharted. And the rate of hotel construction on the higher educational Côte d'Azur is cheapening and slowing down. Obviously a different class of person has taken to going there. But on the prominent early pages there is an announcement of a new educational El Dorado on the nursery coast, especially attractive to working mothers. This one we must explore.

The way I see it now, we have national intent to form a fourth stage of education, not by mechanical expansion upwards, following post-war trends, but expansion downwards to the under-fives. That way lies new excitement for those who are determined to see education made fully available for all children at all stages, no matter what social handicaps attend their birth and background. I think this is the most hopeful road towards educational recreation; a milieu in which family and school can meet and transform the upbringing of their children.

There is, in any case, much to welcome in the White Paper for my EPA colleagues and me. Our cartography has been incorporated. The signposts of our *Educational Priority*, Volume 1, have now been put up as government properties. We called for a pre-school programme, and the government promises a Plowden level of provision. We asked for positive discrimination, and 'priority will be given in the early stages of the programme to areas of disadvantage'. We wanted local diagnosis and avoidance of standard national formulae, and 'the government attaches importance to a full assessment of local resources and needs, and will welcome diversity'. We advocated the hybrid vigour of professional nurseries and parent-involved play groups, and the governent will guide and encourage local authorities to equip voluntary groups and provide them with qualified teachers, recognising that 'the maturity and experience [of mothers] are important assets' and that 'nursery education probably offers the best opportunities for enlisting parental understanding and support for what schools are trying to achieve'. We advised further action research on EPA problems, and this is promised in the package.

It all reads like radical excitement. Nevertheless I am fearful and already disappointed. After all, it is not the brochure but the journey for which we wait. The government intends to take us by a very slow train. We are scheduled to reach Plowden in 1981—and Lady Plowden reported in 1967. There is a lot of doubt about who will be on the train. Mrs Thatcher relies too much on demand, and that will come mostly from the suburbs. Positive discrimination is but vaguely signposted. It ought to have been made completely legible. It should be written in terms of precise measurement and an explicit financial formula. It is not enough to refer hopefully to the experience of the urban programme—though phasing and further grant aid only after inspection would indeed be valuable. Finally, too much is left to the local proprietors. Of course we want local diagnosis, but within the framework of firm central criteria for grant aid and a strong central organisation to ensure that the new travellers arrive. This will not happen unless, *inter alia*, there is at least a partial merger between the Thatcher and Keith Joseph companies.

It is an attractive package and I want to go. But I must write for more detail before recommending it to the neighbours.

The Conservative administration came and went in 1974 but the EPA problem remains with us. In the meantime the large debate on the creation of a Britain integrated by consensus as to fairness and equality in the distribution of social goods and services has continued. In that debate further blows have been struck against the older optimism which thought of education as perhaps the single most important instrument for he creation of an egalitarian society. I argued the limits of an educational approach to the abolition of poverty and the promotion of equality in volume 1. These limits could never be removed by any kind of EPA policy. But on the other hand the raising of educational standards for the most disadvantaged ought to command our attention and energy for its own sake, whether or not it has a powerful impact on the distribution of income, status and opportunities for mobility—a set of objectives which can be reached only by a much broader range of social policies.

5

E. MIDWINTER *Towards a solution of the EPA problem: the community school*

About the time of the governmental scandals of 1973 an article appeared in the *News of the World* about 'Priority', our centre in Liverpool for urban community education and the successor to the 1968–71 Educational Priority Area Project. My colleagues and I had not been inspired by those exorbitant aristocratic examples, nor had our private lives degenerated, to adapt insurance argot, from legal and general to commercial union. It was a rather more humdrum piece on our school-based activities, and it included the somewhat misleading phrase 'his new method of teaching is called Priority'.

The following day a lady rang me from Widnes about her fourteen-year-old son. He had educational difficulties, she explained, and could I conduct, by correspondence, my 'new method' with and for him, that his educating ratings might improve. She had evidently read her Sunday paper with an embarrassing literalness, believing 'Priority' to be something akin to a Charles Atlas course, refreshed with which her son might increase his muscular IQ capacity, so that the eggheads would no longer kick the intellectual sand into his eyes on the academic beach.

I regret I had to tell her—as we must tell everyone—that we have no simple blueprint nor any set of ready-made answers for the problem of the urban child in the urban school in the urban area. The school is not like a pianola, upon which you place a pre-processed perforated roll and just keep pedalling. All one can offer is a frame of reference, laboriously assembled, modified and refined over five years of practical endeavour in Liverpool. Teachers, educationists and others must judge their own situation against this frame of reference, and act and adapt accordingly. Our suggested overall solution is the community school, and it is a golden rule of community education that it is different rather than the same. The chief message is that schools must tailor their educational fittings according to the texture of the cloth of the children and communities they serve.

In the past we have attempted to lay on a *uniform* system of education, into which everyone enters and, according to his or her lights, performs at this or that level before rejoining society. But once one notes and accepts that inequality of circumstances brings children penalised or otherwise to the portals of that system, its justification cracks. Further, when one notes and accepts that the conditions of home and neighbourhood continue throughout to play a vital part in the child's education, then the justification crumbles. It is the continuing factor of the home and community context—as well as the actual being it produces for introduction into the school system—which is so crucial. It requires teachers to accept, humbly, the wretched truth that home and neighbourhood dictate and that schools affirm. We must reverse the conventionally held equation of school and home. We once believed the school to be the 'educator', with help mustered, if we were lucky, from the home. Now we must accept that, for good or ill, the home is the 'educator', and the school gets into the act where it can.

Given a multivariant society, served by a singular (in character) education system, it is scarcely surprising that the twain meet only sporadically, that is, where the culture of the school and the culture of the home are in harmony. Thus we tend to offer children *uniformity* rather than *equality* of opportunity. But, as what we now recognise as the highly crucial home/neighbourhood feature varies considerably, it follows that we require differential education treatments to align with varying communities in order to produce equality. We must, in Aristotle's famous aphorism, treat 'unequals unequally' that educational equality may prevail.

The historical significance of the Halsey report is that it unreservedly and bluntly states, even proclaims this paradox. Other reports had hinted at the inherent irony of schooling, but the Halsey report brooks of no compromise.

There is an impressive irony in the work of the EPA projects. Asked to prepare a policy for urban schools, its answer is: the school cannot repair the ravages of society. Whatever educational opportunities you offer a child, without corresponding *rapport* in his home and neighbourhood he is, by and large, lost. The sincere, if naive, belief that education is the open sesame to life's rich feast dies hard. It may be the menu, but it is not the actual banquet. Along with this goes the idea that as soon as there are signs of social unrest the schools will put it to rights inexpensively and briskly. So there is an enormous residual faith in the school as an agent of change—social reformers hoping to educate for a better life, authoritarians hoping to educate for discipline and self-reliance, parents simply hoping to give their youngsters a good start. We have—we must—explode the myth. Schools are not change agents; they are agents of affirmation.

They confirm what has already been decided by the accident of birth. On the face of it, a secondary school in the centre of a large city must look, in terms of results, like a training school at worst for the unemployed and the juvenile delinquent, at best for the unskilled labourer. On the face of it, Eton must look like a seminary for Foreign Secretaries. Occasionally one still meets people who believe that things actually occur in this manner, that is, that somehow a school like Eton can transform an ordinary schoolboy into a Foreign Secretary, rather like a legendary magician changing a frog into a princess, or, of course (to avoid any charge of prejudice against ordinary schoolboys), vice versa. Obviously the school in these extreme cases has little or no effect on the situation. They rubber-stamp an inevitability. The inner city school can no more avoid the catastrophes of unemployment or bad housing than the public school can avoid the disasters of our Cabinet Ministers.

Life is not, for the majority, a mystery tour. It is a well programmed route and—given that the prognostications one can make unfortunately include, for this majority, the fate of their children—it is a spiralling route. It is this 'city circular' that constitutes what Sir Keith Joseph rightly called the 'cycle of deprivation'. Indeed, life, in this sense, is more akin to the tram than the bus:

There once was a man who said 'Damn!
I suddenly see what I am.
I'm a creature that moves
In predestinate grooves.
I'm not even a bus, I'm a tram.'

Of course, some of the trams have nice, and not all of them have nasty, destinations. The point is the predictability of the journey for everyone, for better or for worse, and the fact that, thus far, education has not shifted the situation unduly. Many examples rehearse the truth of what the Pirates of Penzance might have termed 'a most ingenious paradox'.

Recently I attempted to analyse the social class breakdown of all English and Welsh county boroughs and align that factor with percentage sixth-form and university places. Come variations of staffing and expenditure, come selection or comprehension, the social class factor remains the safest indicator. For instance, some towns—Darlington, Lincoln, Leeds, Reading, Gloucester—have much the same social class pattern as the country at large; and they almost exactly replicate the national averages for sixth-form places and higher education entries. Indeed, Liverpool—sometimes criticised for not doing as well as other 'big' cities in educational achievement—does slightly better than its fellows on the same social class latitude, namely, Teesside, Salford, Wigan and Stoke.

Yet one still insists on concentrating all our effort on changing and increasing the school facilities—one supports this enthusiastically. But it is not enough. No matter how much you do *inside* the school, you can make virtually no impact at all without the informed support of the home. Educational performance, whatever you do, is inevitably linked with social and economic circumstances. What is the one component that is missing, the one element that has not been tried? It is the home—the family and the peer group and the neighbourhood. These, whether we like it or not, are the true and influential educators; we ignore them at our peril. I do not just mean the happy social relations enjoyed by many teachers and many parents—we must build on that. Phase one is over. We showed on the EPA projects—or teachers and parents showed us—that we have two great factors in our favour: we have sympathetic, gifted, devoted teachers and we have concerned, enthusiastic and willing parents. Informal social *rapport* is strong; educational communion is less so, as witness our parental survey. A very large percentage of the school was doing fine and teachers were easy to get to know; a large percentage of parents and children had no clue about method or what the school was actually trying to do.

It is high time for phase two, that is, making home–school relations educationally productive. Let us draw the parent into the dialogue, not so much as a teaching aide, rather as a partner, even a learner, in the process. I am not talking about do-goodery or even about social work as such, with teachers helping families to resolve domestic and other problems. The dual myth of the parents who couldn't care less and the parents who are waiting to pounce and take over should be abandoned, or at least we should accept that a huge proportion are concerned and willing to help. We must state it as strongly as we are able that the successful *professional* teachers must be the ones who understand the need to encompass the parent and the child in the professional teaching relationship. We must suggest that those staff-room hardknocks, with their neo-realistic thumbs stuck in their neo-realistic waistcoats, talking of feet on the ground and knocking some sense into them, are as unrealistic and as unprofessional as the pseudo-idealists in the staff rooms, all twittering pseudo-idealistic fingers and twittering pseudo-idealistic thumbs. We must move beyond the cosy practices of home–school relations and, in a phrase, get down to a hard, solid campaign of parental education, that our children may be better educated.

What must be made clear is that the problem is lack of know-how rather than lack of interest. It is compounded by the insufficiency of the time and energy of parents, who are living under all kinds of stress—mental, emotional, ethnic, physical—in overcrowded conditions with under-employment and all the other badges of social and economic deterioration. There are schools where perhaps over a third of the children come from families dislocated by desertion, death or other causes. There are single-parent families, living in one or two rooms, possibly with poor heating and cooking facilities, maybe with the mother working long hours cleaning or washing up. It is difficult in those circumstances to find time and energy to devote onself to the esoteric delights of Diene's Apparatus or Creativity. And that leads to yet a further compounding of the problem. The EPA parent is almost always one who knew himself or herself the alienation from the school system betokened by non-comprehension and failure. Since their time in school the abracadabra, the mystique and the magical potions have been expanded briskly, so much so that the EPA parent might spread his hands in bewilderment and say, 'How could I possibly help you, the teacher, with your talk of Cuisenaire and Phonics?'

We have recently mounted parental advisory services at the Butlin's holiday centres with mobile shops, promenading prams, a well placed office and thousands of leaflets and hand-outs. In five days, and apart from the general buttonholing, chatting, climate-raising side, a team of four can exhaust themselves with no fewer than 160 separate queries taking half an hour or so to begin to resolve. We have demonstrated a great need for urgent assistance of this third-party nature, but our enthusiasm is muted by the harrowing character of this need. The teams have been shocked by the number and profundity and gravity of the queries: they felt that they were only scratching at the surface; they felt that the modes for helping parents are normally woefully frail. One or two came from outside—paid 80p to get into the camp as day visitors, having travelled from Blackburn to Pwhelli, for example, because they knew an advisory service was available. And these are not EPA parents, they are much more the solid artisan families from the well established echelons of upper working-class and lower middle-class prosperity. Even so, there were 160 queries out of 10,000 visitors—including, remember, 4,000 children. Maybe there were 2,000 families represented here. And that was just a beginning. What does it mean conceivably in terms of the nation? Might it mean that, out there, there is one family in every thirty-six at any time with a major educational problem) Not just, like everyone else, a need to be acquainted with the day by day process of education, but a pertinent query.

But what concern and interest that, during a holiday, so many people should leave the swimming pools and bingo sessions anxiously to enquire after their children's educational well-being. On the other hand, we did a snap educational awareness survey with a hundred families. Only thirty-nine knew the name of the Secretary of State for Education, sixty-six the normal infant–junior transfer age, twelve what i.t.a. meant and fifty-three what the 'O' in 'O' level stood for.

No one would suggest that there is much mileage in knowing these things in themselves, but it is an indicator of know-how. Education, moreover, is a hidden problem, especially in the EPAs. You know when you are unemployed, or when your housing is sub-standard, or when your welfare benefits are up the pole. Because of the zealous devotion and professional tenacity of teachers and educational administrators the schools are about the only part of the system that actually works. Come age five years or nine o'clock in the morning, and the parents, often thankfully, can hand over their children into the welcoming bosom of the school until, respectively, sixteen years or four o'clock. No other service performs its task so pleasantly and efficiently, and here one must pay a tribute to the diligence, the dedication and the determination of the EPA teacher, who has the most exacting teaching job in the country and accomplishes it with great credit and skill. Yet, given this overtly excellent service, we have to persuade parents that their contribution is crucial, and that the child is in school only five hours a day. By sixteen the youngster has lived 140,000 hours, of which only 10,000, or one in fourteen, have been spent in school.

The EPA projects have taken one and a half of the two necessary steps. There is that first phase of enlisting this very definite parental concern and mobilising it for the support of the child. This phase we may confidently claim we have completed. We have deployed a number of tactical variations for establishing an informed dialogue and communion between home and school—what amounts, in fact, to a public relations campaign. We have perhaps exorcised for ever that persistent hobgoblin of teacher demonology the feckless, apathetic working-class parent by demonstrating that they will, provided with the right stimulus, respond magnificently. The second phase is not complete, but it is promising; namely, the effective utilisation of this parental force—ensuring that it does have a valid effect on the child's education. Partly because we put the horse before the cart (we had to get the parents involved before we could measure their impact) and partly because it needs a longer and more intense period of evaluation the actual evidence in this second phase is smaller but very heartening.

All this means that we have taken a step beyond the vogue use of 'compensatory education' so-called, which accepts that the education system is fine but that, for some children at some points in society, there is a need for souped-up treatments to 'compensate' for purported 'deficits' in the children's make-ups. We are establishing the point firmly that case studies of individual children are well nigh useless in a social vacuum. They are useful, but notably when the context is conducive to such activity. That is, all the possible relationships in and across the community need to be built up as an amenable base upon which the child may be educationally developed. This means that the community school will vary accordingly as it probes the weaknesses and reinforces the strengths of its catchment area. We have introduced into the concept of 'positive discrimination' the meaningful idea of 'local diagnosis'. Before we pour, as we should, massive extra resources into disadvantaged districts we must carefully analyse the incidence and depth of need and potential in the given area, so that the community school will be completely in tune with its locality. Theoretically these are twin sophistications of educational action, with community, or complementary, education and local diagnosis being modifications or projections of compensatory education and positive discrimination.

Of course, there is no point in running an 'open' school with lots of welcomes for the parents if the curriculum of the school is not in keeping. Briefly, we preach the idea of socially relevant curricula for the community school, based on the psychologically sound theory of rooting children's development in their immediate experience and, at the same time, attempting to prepare them to adjust to, cope with and, hopefully, control their social environment when they are citizens. This is the aim of the community school. Not only do we expect that the backing of the home and neighbourhood will assist the school, we anticipate that, in the longer term, the school will aid the community to solve its own problems. This is the celebrated interaction of community education. But there is an important subsidiary to the socially or community-orientated curriculum, and one we have seen in our child–parent projects, which operates in action. We have constantly found that if the curriculum is related to the community in these ways, then it gives parents the assurance to come forward and assist. They are half-way there. They understand the problems under consideration only too well, having learned them in the hard school of experience, and this gives them the confidence to join in the learning process in a wholehearted manner. This is the other side of the medallion. The school invites the parents to come half-way to meet them; the school—by altering its curriculum, its structures and its attitudes—must go half-way to meet the parent. Only in this way can the educational nexus be created in which the child can profitably develop.

But it is mainly a question of everyone taking up cudgels and developing the idea, begun in many places, of entering into a one-to-one correspondence with a child or a family for the betterment of its educational attainment. We need a high standard of professionalism in all we do for parents—journals, leaflets, hand-outs, demonstrations, exhibitions and expositions of all kinds—and all the media must be brought more into play—radio and television, especially of a local variety but particularly the press and other journals. Where, for educational queries, are the equivalent of the gardening, health and lovesick columns found in so many newspapers and magazines? We need all possible advertising techniques, and these should be negotiated nationally by the DES as large-scale campaigns, utilising everything from TV commercials to milk-bottle covers and matchboxes. We need all possible asisstance for schools from every possible source as teachers begin to step up their home–school firepower. We need fleets of mobile advisory vans and vehicles, moving from house to house and location to location, maintaining a consistent presence of educational information and know-how. We need every conceivable type of advisory service for every conceivable kind of spot from holiday camp to factory canteen, from library to laundrette. We need adult education provision of any unorthodox or unconventional kind which will help pull off the trick of improving the neighbourhood educational quotient. We need to develop kits and sets of material for home usage at every educational stage. We need sound, outgoing and positive educational advice freely proffered and something akin to an educational Ombudsman counselling and assessing and resolving problems down at district level. At the hub of this would be the Educational Visitor, whose job might well be as generator and mobiliser of those strengths and reserves of energy in the community itself. For when we have finished pouring in all these directives and officers and so on it is the educational health of the community itself which will make or break the effect of the campaign. It is the mothers and fathers who matter. Initially the Educational Visitors and all the others must educate and train cadres of paramilitary mums and dads who, after introductory inductions and courses, may begin to spread the know-how to their friends, relations and mates, fanning out the skills and information in ever-extending circles of parental concern and commitment. To recall the war cry coined by Herbert Morrison in World War II, it is a case of 'Up, housewives, and at 'em'.

The term Educational Visitor is used deliberately and advisedly. It is intended to recall the health visitor, who, over the turn of the century and since, has helped transmit a huge body of medical knowledge to the laity. What might be termed the 'physical' education of the nation has been considerably enhanced over the last sixty or so years. All manner of medical 'mysteries' have become part of the common lore which mother passes on to daughter. It is with an effort that one remembers that all the information about diet, vitamins, hygiene, nappies, colic and all the assorted ways and means of rearing the young child were once closely held professional secrets. Now it is the turn of the teacher similarly to share his mystique with the parents. It is the turn of the educationists to take the laity into their confidence and unfold the secrets of the teaching art.

This should not mean any decline in the status of the teacher. We have assuredly not seen any such drop in the prestige of the medical profession this century. Rather it might improve his status as the teacher becomes the professional convenor of the educative community. He would be somewhat like the conductor of an orchestra, in this case the educative orchestra, leading and guiding that interactive dimension of social life which affects educational analysis, objectives and implementation.

And there is another sense in which health can point out a valuable analogy. In the nineteenth century we were slow to see how ill health

interlocked with poverty and crime, and slower yet to see how ignorance interconnected with the other three. Again in the twentieth
century, as different manifestations of ill health, poverty and crime
have made themselves felt, we have been a trifle faltering in our
recognition of the interconnections, and once more the relationship of
this mesh of social ills with ignorance has not been too swiftly
remarked. The Halsey report pointed the way to a proper perspective
for education. It is an issue of the individual, but of the individual in
his total community. Just as we seek to succour the citizen from
cradle to grave for the good of his health, so we must do the same for
education. We succour his health in its composite social context, and
we do so both for his own good and for the benefit of the community.
Now we must see 'education' in a similar way. We must view it not
just as a childlike, school-like thing but as a factor permeating the
whole of the community, and with the teacher's responsibility to that
community total and remorseless. Like health, education is a complete
dimension of life; it is a climate of opinion and activity within society,
not just the peddling of often outdated facts to children for a few
years of their young lives.

The ramifications of this concept for the role of the teacher are
tremendous, and there is no point in shying away from them. It is a
quite fundamental change, and no one should try to pretend it would
be pointless. It first suggests that the teacher should be a social critic,
or at least be imbued with a positively heightened awareness of the
community context in which he is working. The strengths and
weaknesses, the needs and the characteristics of his community base
must be known intimately to him so that he can guide his pupils and
(where, in turn, their role impinges on the educative community) the
citizenry in a dispassionate and constructive appraisal of their
situation. The traditional role of the teacher has been socially defensive rather than neutral, let alone offensive, in the sense of a social
critique, and society itself must come to understand that the teacher's
task is to equip children so that they can come independently to their
own terms with their own destiny apropos their own values.

Perhaps more important in the short term, the teacher must also
come to include adult education as a major part of his professional
skills. If the unit of treatment is the parent-plus-the-child rather than,

as in the past, the child in a vacuum, then it is imperative that the teacher has the skills to relate professionally with adults as well as with the child. The repercussions on teacher training would be most significant, for at the moment many colleges are not well prepared to handle this problem. Indeed, we find that over the last five years the mood has changed from teachers arguing strongly that their job is to get the children *away* from their mothers in order to raise standards, to teachers agreeing that the principle of parental engagement is correct but complaining that they have not been furnished with the requisite skills.

However, if the teacher thus became social critic and adult educator he would, by that token, become a community craftsman. He would be a professional serving the educational community, not because of some obtuse idealogical zaniness but because moral precepts of social justice combine with the sheer staring-you-in-the-face, practical horse-sensical facts of the educational situation to make it essential so to do. Whatever one's goals, whether they are conventional ones of academic achievement or the more avant-garde ones of social involvement, the key to successful practice must comprehend an effective dialogue with the home. And as for the few teachers who would still reject parents, it is frightening to recall that those parents were purportedly educated, some of them a matter of only a few years ago, by the teachers who now deem them dangerous. 'You cannot help us,' they seem to imply, 'because we failed you.'

All in all, the parental component is the one major missing link which needs to be joined and maintained if we are anxious to reap a significant advance towards educational equality. We have, until recently, confused equality and uniformity. All children have enjoyed, technically, a uniform chance in our rather rigid and 'singular' educational system. But ours is a multivariant society, which means an inexhaustible permutation of 'educative communities', at work, whether we like it or not, dictating a child's educational chances. The lesson of the successful middle-class or suburban school is not 'Go ye and do likewise' in disadvantaged working-class environs. The lesson of such a school is that it enjoys an interflow of values, language and so on with its catchment neighbourhood. By promoting the concept of the school community we would hope that some children would develop more critical skills in order to examine more opportunities so as to make more independent and more unfettered decisions about their destinations in life. The core of the so-called disadvantage is ultimately about limited choice; it is about people inhibited, by whatever reason, from choosing their own life style. By developing schools that gell with their attendant communities, and in particular the parents within those communities, one might hope, not so much to bring children to the starting line equal, but to bring more children to the finishing line equal.

6

A. N. LITTLE *The performance of children from ethnic minority backgrounds in primary schools*

The issues

Over the past twenty years the characteristics of the school population in certain local education authorities have changed with the arrival of immigrants to this country from the New Commonwealth. Their children (those who arrived with their parents, those who came later, and, more recently, growing numbers born in this country) have needs in common with other pupils, and they also have special needs stemming partly from the fact of their or their parents' recent arrival and partly from cultural differences, as well as specific language needs. On top of this there is the majority population's reactions to them and in particular their colour. (CRC, 1974.) The key issue facing educationalists is the extent to which the conventional educational system and its practices require modification to ensure equality of opportunity and performance for these pupils and ways in which necessary modifications can be best achieved. (*Ibid.*)

At the outset two major points must be emphasised:

1 Although pupils with 'New Commonwealth' backgrounds constitute a small proportion of the total school population in the country as a whole, their concentration is such that in certain areas—especially urban areas—they account for a large propor-

tion of the relevant population. Townsend (1972) has shown, for example, that these pupils constituted 3·3 per cent of the total school population in the country on the basis of the Department of Education and Science definition; and he calculated that on a wider definition the figure is about 4·5 per cent. This small proportion, however, conceals the uneven distribution The London area accounts for slightly more than half, followed by south Lancashire and the west Midlands. In fact two local authority areas have more than 25 per cent of their pupil roll defined as immigrant, five between 20 and 25 per cent and a further six 15–20 per cent. Furthermore the number of individual schools with heavy concentrations is growing. Nearly 1,000 schools out of 33,000 now have over a quarter immigrant pupils, and some authorities with few children of minority groups overall have one or two schools with very large percentages. This uneven distribution means that some areas and schools are faced with a greater need to cope with the educational issues which pupils from minority backgrounds present than others, and in these areas a twofold response is called for. The first requirement is a commitment to positive policies, an admission that the education of minority group children is an important issue, a move away from the 'we have no problems here' approach found in some areas. Secondly the need is for more resources to be made available to such areas, both from the local education authorities and as a result of positive action by central government.

2   A second consideration which is relevant concerns the extent to which the educational needs of these pupils and those of underprivileged sections of the indigenous community are similar (Halsey, 1972). Similarities exist because many with New Commonwealth backgrounds live in depressed areas with whites; further, some of them share the characteristics of the socially and economically disadvantaged groups in society. Yet these similarities do not override important differences. For one thing, not all recent settlers come from economically disadvantaged homes, nor do they all reside in depressed areas. Beyond this, two important factors must be recognised. Firstly the different ethnic background of these settlers and the fact that they do not share

the common English language heritage sets them apart from the indigenous community. Their values, attitudes and behaviour differ in important respects from those of the indigenous population; and it should be possible to preserve these differences. Secondly, because of their colour they are a visible minority and are often subject to the hostility of the host community as well as frequent discrimination in such areas as housing and employment. Furthermore the low economic and social status which New Commonwealth immigrants are frequently accorded in our society must affect the 'identity' these groups have of themselves and the self concept they can pass on to their children. These factors determine the character of the educational issues which emerge in the schools and must, in turn, influence the responses which the schools and local authorities adopt, and it is in view of these factors that such educational issues require serious consideration in their own right.

It is tempting in finding answers to points like these to look across the atlantic to United States experience. But how far does the current American urban racial situation provide a portent for the United Kingdom (Little, 1974)? Initially it is important to point the differences between the two situations:

Size. Clearly there is no comparison in the relative size and concentrations of racial minority populations in the United Kingdom and United States. Well over 20 million Americans are black, and this is one American in eight or nine, compared with an estimated 1½ million 'coloured' in the United Kingdom, or less than 3 per cent of the population. Many American cities are anticipating that well over half their population will be black by the mid-1980s (and the list includes areas like metropolitan New York, Chicago, Philadelphia, St Louis, Detroit, Cleveland, Oakland, Baltimore and New Orleans), and already Washington DC, Newark and Gary have metropolitan populations of over 50 per cent black. Public school populations of most of these cities are already over half black, and in Washington DC less than one pupil in twenty in the public schools is white. This contrasts with the United Kingdom situation. It was impossible a decade ago to find even census enumeration districts that were exclusively black;

currently only two of our local education authorities have more than a quarter of their pupils defined as 'immigrant', and a further four between a fifth and a quarter classified in the same way. Although two out of three West Indian children are in schools in the Greater London area and half in the inner city area (ILEA), few schools have concentrations of the minority groups implied in the United States figure. In the ILEA area 60 per cent of so-called immigrant pupils are in schools with less than 20 per cent immigrants, and only one immigrant pupil in six is in a school with over 50 per cent immigrants. In the whole country fewer than 150 schools had more than 50 per cent of their pupils defined as immigrant in 1971.

Homogeneity. Although the United States' minority population is not exclusively Negro, during recent discussions about both race and urban problems the difficulties of Puerto Rican, Asian as well as European immigrants have been given little emphasis. By contrast the United Kingdom settler population is highly differentiated. Again using education figures, of 270,450 pupils defined as "immigrant" in 1971 40 per cent were of West Indian origin, 20 per cent Indian, 10 per cent Pakistani and a further 10 per cent from Africa. All these groups might be defined as black. The importance of this point is that the reasons the parents of these children had for coming to this country, the experiences they brought with them and their adjustment to the host environment are different. Of particular significance is the extent to which they bring with them a transferable and viable culture of their own, different from and independent of the dominant white culture. Certainly the African and Asian populations have retained most of their own cultural identity even in the United Kingdom, which contrasts markedly with he disorganised situation of many American blacks, whose culture is largely that of the dominant and rejecting white majority: how far the settlers from the Caribbean have an autonomous cultural identity and how far they are in a similar situation to the American Negro is debatable. Certainly one of the educational issues require urgent consideration is the extent to which the school by its staffing policies (i.e. employing black professionals) and curricula can assist in the development of a black identity and help preserve the cultural identity of minority groups. Recent settlers to the United Kingdom are internally differentiated. Initially (and sensibly) it is possible to distinguish them by country of origin, but even these national origins are cut across by rural and urban differences, class and colour distinctions in their country of origin. The Asian population provides an example of this diversity, but no less important are the differences between settlers from the West Indian islands, and even within islands immigrants from rural and urban areas and with different shades of blackness have different attitudes towards their own and other people's skin colour.

History. The American black is an internal migrant, until a generation or two ago the inferior member of the southern plantation society. Migration to the cities was always a way out of a social system that in many respects paralleled caste society, with the blacks being universally considered second-class citizens. Industrialisation in the northern cities and the war economy enormously widened the opportunities for the black population and chances for migrating north. But in essence many of the urban blacks are still living in the shadow of the slave plantations in a way in which settlers in the United Kingdom have never been dominated by the cultural and economical standards of the whites. Even in the West Indies domination of blacks by whites was never as severe as in the United States (one illustration of the fact is that some of the leaders of recent black militantism in the United States had their origins not in the ghettoes of the United States cities nor in the American south but in the West Indies), and a major reason for this was that both in the West Indies and in Asia the whites were always outnumbered by the blacks. As a result a black bourgeoisie was always in evidence. Further, a peculiar mixture of missionary zeal and transient colonial exploitation gave the relationship between whites and blacks in the West Indies a different flavour from its counterparts in the United States. The capacity of the Asian culture(s) to withstand the pressures of commercial, political and religious colonisation is legendary; resilience is a word that has frequently been used to describe the capacity of Asians to preserve a cultural integrity and identity against colonisation. As a result the settlers in the United Kingdom do not present the same kind or degree of either cultural disorganisation or perhaps the same need to see themselves through white eyes and standards as do American blacks. The phrase American blacks was an apt description of the situation of the Negro in the United States in a way that black or brown British is not accurate for the first generation of settlers in the United Kingdom.

Institutional framework. A further difference between the countries is the institutional framework within which race relations take place and which structure the economy and social opportunities and life styles of minority populations. The different relationship between central, regional and local authorities in the United States and the United Kingdom inevitably means that problems and opportunities differ. The fact that nearly one third of housing in the United Kingdom is controlled by public bodies and therefore within the public domain means that the public policy (in this case local authority policy) could (if one wanted it to) have a profound effect on the housing opportunities of smaller and minority groups. The fact that the State is a major employer not only in the bureaucratic sense of the civil service but directly in industrial sectors like mines, public utilities and steel, services like transport, post and telecommunications, means that public recruitment, training and promotion policies could directly change the employment situation of minorities and serve as an example to private employers. Finally, parallel with the migration control of the 1960s came a legal framework for race relations. This included legislation against incitement to race hatred, discrimination in employment, housing and recreational facilities and the creation of a framework for the encouragement of harmonious community relations. The positive effort to discourage discrimination was established within a decade of the arrival of sizable numbers of black settlers in this country. This contrasts with the United States situation, in which legislation and action against discrimination and inequality were imposed upon set conventions and behaviour that had been established generations previously.

Commitment to change. So far the bulk of the argument suggests that the United States and the United Kingdom problems are different in their scale, history and ease of amelioration. There is an important respect where this is not only an oversimplification but also distorts the situation, namely the commitment to a positive effort for changing the situation and the mobilisation of sufficient resources to achieve some effect. The cost of the British urban programme (which was explicitly stated not to be an immigrant programme, although it is the only major programme for assisting areas where immigrants have settled in large numbers) between January 1969 and November 1971 was £18 million, and the extension of the programme until 1976 brought the provision of funds up to £40 million. Contrast this with the estimates for the first year of the anti-poverty programme in the United States of $1 billion. In so far as willingness to mobilise resources is a measure of commitment to change, there can be little doubt about the relative seriousness of the United States and United Kingdom efforts. For example, the Community Relations Commission budget in the United Kingdom is currently around £1 million. One project to assess the impact of negative income tax on minorities in the United States received twice as much.

Because of these points the easy comparisons with the United States should be attempted only with care, and not as an alternative to undertaking detailed examination of the United Kingdom situation.

One point should not be lost sight of in this examination as far as the school population is concerned. In the late '50s and early '60s virtually all Asian and West Indian pupils were born and frequently started their education outside the United Kingdom. During the second half of the '60s the number of minority group pupils born in this country increased. By the end of the '70s virtually all black pupils in primary schools and an increasing proportion in secondary schools will have been born here. This means that the nature of the educational issues will change. One aspect of this is the type of cultural conflict and clash that is created for a black person simultaneously living in the majority world of school and the minority world of home. In principle the problem is common to all minority groups; in practice its nature and intensity will differ between groups.

Opportunity

For some people the arrival of large numbers of black settlers was seen exclusively as a problem or series of problems. Schools and their staffs were sometimes guilty of the same stereotyped 'problem' view.

There is little doubt that new issues were raised and old problems intensified by the presence of black pupils in schools and in the community, but equally important (and often neglected) are the opportunities proffered by their presence. The presence of 1½ million black people in Britain does not make it a multi-racial society either in the numerical sense (it is actually 3 per cent of the total population) nor in the strictly scientific sense (it would be inappropriate to see the various minority groups in this country as racial or race groups), but what is beyond doubt is that areas and schools with ethnic minorities have the opportunity of creating the conditions within which equal relationships can exist between groups and equal opportunities can be proffered to minority groups. To achieve this would be no mean achievement and would require a widening perspective on the educational experiences of pupils from majority backgrounds. The United Kingdom has become more differentiated by the presence of a black community(ies). In consequence the educational experience offered to the majority population should be modified and in certain respects radially changed to enable them to cope adequately with the facts of cultural, national and racial diversity. Clearly this implies changes in the curricula and teaching methods, not least important eliminating the xenophobia and cultural blinkers that permeate much history, geography and literature teaching.

Sources of school performance

It must be emphasised that the findings reported in this paper do not indicate the potentiality of children from minority groups; they are based upon conventional tests of performance within the existing primary schools and therefore they are culturally limited in two senses:

1 They are related to the traditional primary school curriculum and are largely concerned with basic skill acquisition: reading, English and mathematics.
2 The tests themselves, and especially the reading and verbal tests, require various cultural experiences (in and out of school) in order for the pupil to perform adequately upon them. Such experiences may have been denied to many minority group pupils.

What these test results do indicate is the performance of pupils from a minority background within the existing school system, and results from three separate sources are reported:

A

An analysis of the distribution of performance of 4,269 'immigrants'[1] and 22,023 non-immigrants entering secondary schools in the autumn of 1968. At that time all pupils in the ILEA due to transfer to secondary schools were placed in one of seven 'profile' groups for English mathematics and verbal reasoning (a separate group for each subject) by the primary school. For English and mathematics the primary school ranked its own pupils in order of merit and provisionally assigned each to a group. Each child was then tested in the two subjects anonymously in the school. The tests were marked in the school and the results collated centrally. Schools were then informed of the number of pupils who, compared with all pupils in the authority, would be expected to fall into each of the seven groups. In the light of this information the Head then made his final decision on the groups to be assigned to each pupil. The procedure for verbal reasoning was different. Pupils took probably two standardised tests in the autumn term, and in January all pupils took the same test, which was marked by the school. A conversion table was provided for converting numerical marks into the seven groups. The Head then decided the group for each pupil, using the test results and his own assessment of the pupil's ability. Theoretically 10 per cent of the pupils should be in group 1, 15 per cent in group 2, 15 per cent in group 3, 20 per cent in group 4, 15 per cent in group 5, 15 per cent in group 6 and 10 per cent in group 7. For the purposes of this report the survey will be called survey or project A. (LEA report, unpublished.)

B

An analysis of the reading standards of 32,000 pupils in the first term

---

[1] The definition of immigrant is the DES one, i.e. an immigrant pupil is a child either (*a*) born outside the United Kingdom but now living with parents, relatives or guardians in the country or (*b*) born inside the United Kingdom to parents whose country of origin was abroad and who have been in the United Kingdom for less than about ten years. (The definition excludes those from Northern Ireland and Eire.)

of their second-year junior schooling in October 1968 in the ILEA. The test used was a sentence completion test (involving silent reading and comprehension) devised by the NFER for their streaming project. Several points must be made about the test. It was a group test and not an individual one, and inevitably a relatively blunt measure of reading attainment. Further, it measured reading comprehension and not other aspects of literacy (reading fluency, oracy, etc). Other basic primary skills (writing and numeracy) have been ignored, as have other aspects of the curriculum (social adjustment and personal relationships). More varied and comprehensive testing might have produced different results. For the purpose of this paper it is necessary either to assume a high correlation between the reading skill measured by the test used and other cognitive skills and/or that the reading skill is of such intrinsic importance that the results are of intrinsic interest. This survey will be called survey or project B. (Little and Mabey, 1973.)

C

One of the areas used as part of the national Educational Priority Area Project was in central London, and amongst the information collected about pupils were the following measures of performance:

(a) A test of reading standards (SRA).
(b) A test of passive vocabulary (English Picture Vocabulary Test).
(c) A test of psycho-linguistic functioning (Illinois Test of Psycholinguistic Abilities).
(d) A test of basic skill performance in primary schools (Bristol Achievement Tests).

In all, 3,000 pupils attended the schools in the area and the schools were recognised by both the DES and the ILEA as EPA schools (e.g. teachers in seven of the twelve schools received the £75 allowance for teachers in EPA schools, and all were included in the ILEA's own schemes to aid EPA schools). As one pupil in six was defined as an immigrant, the results provided an unique opportunity to compare performance of underprivileged and immigrant pupils. This study will be referred to as survey or project C.

Results

Immigrant performance and length of education (source: survey *A*). Table 6.1 shows how far the performance distributions of all immigrants were markedly different from both the theoretical and actual ILEA distributions. For example, fewer immigrants than expected

TABLE 6.1

Performance of pupils at transfer to secondary school

	English		Mathematics		Verbal reasoning	
Distribution	% 1 + 2	% 6 + 7	% 1 + 2	% 6 + 7	% 1 + 2	% 6 + 7
Theoretical	25	25	25	25	25	25
Non-immigrants	25·0	23·2	22·9	25·6	19·8	28·9
Immigrants	8·1	53·0	8·0	53·5	6·7	58·9
West Indian	5·0	57·9	3·8	61·6	3·6	66·6
Indians/Pakistani	14·1	44·9	16·2	42·2	13·4	48·4
Greek Cypriot	8·1	50·3	10·1	46·1	5·9	55·6
Turkish Cypriot	2·2	65·2	4·7	64·8	3·5	70·0
Other immigrant	15·3	41·6	15·2	37·5	12·9	41·6
Long-stay	12·4	37·9	11·7	41·5	10·0	46·1
Short-stay	5·5	61·8	6·0	60·6	4·7	66·8

were placed in the top two groups (e.g. 8 per cent on the English) and more in the bottom two groups (53 per cent), compared with an expected 25 per cent. The performance distributions of the non-immigrants, on the other hand, were either the same as or better than expected (more in groups 1 and 2, fewer in 6 and 7). For example, again on the English, 25 per cent of non-immigrants were in groups 1 and 2, 23 per cent in groups 6 and 7. These examples are typical of results on all three tests; the non-immigrants had better distributions than the immigrants.

None of the nationality groups studied had distributions similar to the theoretical or actual ILEA or non-immigrant distributions. Each of the given nationality groups (West Indian, Indian and Pakistani, Greek Cypriot and 'others') had smaller percentages in groups 1 and 2, higher percentages in groups 6 and 7, than the comparative distributions. For example, on the English test these ranged from 2·2 per cent (Turkish Cypriots) to 15·3 per cent ('others') in groups 1 and 2, compared with 25 per cent of the ideal and 23·7 per cent of the actual ILEA. The distribution of the 'others' and Indians/Pakistanis came 'closest' to all the nationality groups, to the theoretical and actual ILEA distributions (i.e. relatively the highest percentages in groups 1 and 2 and the lowest in groups 6 and 7). The opposite was true of the West Indians and the Turkish Cypriots. Greek Cypriots were in the mid-position. On the English test, for example, more than thirty times as many Turkish Cypriots were in groups 6 and 7 as in groups 1 and 2; the West Indians had more than eleven times as many in groups 6 and 7 as in groups 1 and 2, the Greek Cypriots more than six times as many, the Indians/Pakistanis more than three times as many, and the 'others' more than twice as many. For non-immigrant pupils the ratio is roughly 1 : 1. For all but the West Indians the distributions on the mathematics were closest to the non-immigrant distribution. It seems, then, that for pupils from non-English-speaking countries performance was, not surprisingly, best on the least verbal of the tests. Differences between the immigrant groups and the actual ILEA distributions were generally most marked on the verbal reasoning test.

Immigrants who had a full education in the United Kingdom did better than the newly arrived immigrants. On the English, for example, 5·5 per cent of the more recent arrivals were in groups 1 and 2, compared with 12·4 per cent of these who had a full United Kingdom education. Comparative percentages for the bottom two groups were 62 and 38 per cent. It is important to note that distributions of the immigrants with full United Kingdom education were by no means the same as the distributions of the non-immigrants (for example, 25 per cent of the non-immigrants were in the top two groups for English, compared with 12 per cent for long stay). Given the importance attached to the actual process of immigration, it was expected that the long-stay immigrants born here would do better than the long-stay immigrants arriving during infancy. This, however, was not the case; in fact the distributions of those born here and those arriving before the beginning of infant schools (1956–59 or 1960–61) were very similar. Performance on the English may again be taken as an example, as the pattern is the same in mathematics and verbal reasoning. On the English, percentages in groups 1 and 2 varied from 11·8 per cent (1956–59 arrivals) to 12·6 per cent (born here), while percentages in groups 6 and 7 varied from 36·9 per cent (1960–61 arrivals) to 38·4 per cent (born here); in neither case is the difference educationally significant. The critical factor, then, seemed to be the extent of the pupil's education in the United Kingdom. A full education in the United Kingdom seemed most important in determining performance, but even with a full education, the performance of the immigrant was not the same as that of non-immigrant. The relationship between performance and amount of United Kingdom education seemed to be almost linear where the more recent arrivals were concerned; as the amount of the education decreased from 'some infants and full junior school' experience to 'less than one year junior school' percentages placed in groups 1 and 2 decreased, while those in 6 and 7 increased. For example, on the verbal reasoning percentages placed in groups 1 and 2 ranged from 7 per cent (1962–64 arrivals) to 3·6 per cent (1965–67 arrivals) to 2·4 per cent (1968 arrivals).

A further point is worth making about pupils with full education in the United Kingdom: although the distributions of West Indians with a full education in the United Kingdom were better than the distributions of new arrivals, they were still far from the indigenous. Table 6.2 shows that 9 per cent in English and over 7 per cent in mathematics and verbal reasoning were placed in the upper quarter. By contrast the distributions of Indians/Pakistanis with full United

TABLE 6.2

Percentage of pupils fully educated placed in upper quartile on transfer to secondary school

	English	Mathematics	Verbal reasoning
West Indian origin	9·2	7·4	7·2
Asian origin	19·3	20·2	21·1
Indigenous	25	22·9	19·8

Kingdom education were only slightly different from the actual ILEA distributions, around 20 per cent on all three tests placed in the upper quarter.

From this analysis three points should be emphasised:

1 The 'immigrant' population is a heterogeneous one, both in national origin and in performance in primary schools. On the whole, pupils from India and Pakistan do better than other immigrants, and West Indian and Turkish Cypriot children appear to do rather worse.
2 Length of education in the United Kingdom appears to be a more important determinant of performance than length of residence. This finding underlines the existing efforts of school staffs and perhaps suggests the need for pre-school facilities for underprivileged pupils generally and minority pupils in particular.
3 There is a high intercorrelation in performance on all three measures of the primary curriculum

Social and ethnic mix of school and attainment (source: survey B). In this section the effect on reading attainment of children of different social/ethnic backgrounds in schools of varying social and immigrant composition is examined. The attainment data used in this paper are derived from a survey of eight-year-olds, and the measure of attainment used is the mean reading quotient (RQ) for groups and subgroups. The test was standardised on a national sample with a mean of 100, standard deviation of 15 and range of 70–140. The mean RQ for the London survey was 94·4. Mean scores can be very roughly converted into reading ages. A mean score of 90, for example, is equivalent to a reading age roughly two years below chronological age. Overall, London children had a reading age roughly six months behind their chronological age, and immigrants about one year below. When considering the effect on children's attainment of immigrant concentration it is important to examine the effect on the performance of both immigrants and non-immigrants. In order to simplify presentation, non-immigrants and immigrants have been dealt with separately. Furthermore for the non-immigrants I have excluded the Irish and concentrated on children born in the United Kingdom.

Table 6.3 indicates that there is a fairly marked relationship between attainment and immigrant concentration in the school. The

TABLE 6.3

Mean reading score of UK children in schools with varying proportions of immigrants

Percentage of immigrants	UK	
0	99·0	(1,104)
1–10	97·7	(10,578)
10·1–20	95·3	(5,267)
20·1–30	95·6	(2,348)
30·1–40	94·4	(1,440)
40·1–50	96.5	(397)
50·1–60	93·7	(429)
60·1–70	88·9	(73)

total range in attainment between low and high concentration is ten points, which is approximately one year's reading age. There is a fall in attainment of children in schools with more than 60 per cent immigrants; excluding this last group the range is six points, which is equivalent to six months' reading age. But there is not a smooth progression. There is very little difference, for example, in the mean scores of children in schools of between 10 and 50 per cent immigrant concentration, and in fact the mean of the 40–50 group is marginally higher than those of the three previous groups, suggesting that it is the extremes of immigrant concentration (i.e. less than 10 per cent and more than 50 per cent) that is related to the performance of the in-digenous population.

This analysis can be taken a step further by examining the effect on different ethnic groups' mean performance of varying percentage from different socio-economic and other backgrounds. Three impor-tant points emerge from this analysis (see table 6.4). First, for nearly all occupational groups there seems to be a trend of lower perfor-mance with higher immigrant concentration. For most occupational groups a marked fall in performance seems to occur when the im-migrant concentration is greater than 10 per cent, and in schools which have 50 per cent or more immigrants (although this latter is not true of the professional or the semi-skilled groups). Secondly, it should

TABLE 6.4

Mean reading score of UK children, classified by guardian's occupation and school's immigrant concentration

Percentage of immigrants	Professional		Other non-manual		Skilled		Semi-skilled		Unskilled	
<10	109·0	(1,159)	102·0	(1,973)	98·1	(3,800)	94·5	(2,335)	91·9	(2,109)
10·1–30	106·6	(617)	100·1	(1,054)	96·1	(2,579)	92·9	(1,745)	89·8	(1,348)
30·1–50	105·5	(124)	99·4	(288)	95·6	(660)	92·8	(383)	89·6	(308)
>50	104·9	(22)	97·3	(81)	93·7	(159)	93·1	(112)	87·6	(98)

be noted that *within* each occupational group the differences in mean score are not so great as the range shown in table 6.3 (even allowing for the merging of the 60–70 per cent immigrant groups). For most groups the range is the order of four and a half points (except among the semi-skilled, where the range is of one and a half points only). Thirdly, it is worth noting that parental occupation appears to be more important than the immigrant concentration of the school. Further support for this proposition can be obtained from the fact that in most cases a child whose parent is in a high status occupation but is himself in a school of high immigrant concentration attains at a higher level than the child whose parent has a lower (occupational) status but is in a school with few immigrants. One example of this is that the mean score of children of professional parents in schools with more than 50 per cent immigrants is 104·9 while there is a mean score of 102·0 for the children of other non-manual parents who are in schools with under 10 per cent immigrants. It is interesting to note that the effect of immigrant concentration on performance is virtually identical with the effect of lower working-class concentration on the performance of children from different social backgrounds.

TABLE 6.5

Mean reading score of non-immigrant children in schools of varying education priority rank and immigrant concentration

Percentage of immigrants	Education priority rank							
	1		2		3		4	
(a) *Non-manual*								
< 10	97·5	(67)	96·1	(174)	100·2	(613)	106·2	(2,429)
10·1–30	96·6	(77)	99·4	(317)	101·7	(679)	104·8	(737)
30·1–50	94·2	(36)	101·3	(138)	101·2	(224)	103·9	(58)
> 50	96·1	(35)	99·1	(47)	104·1	(17)	—	
(b) *Manual*								
< 10	89·3	(371)	90·2	(712)	93·8	(2,821)	97·0	(4,881)
10·1–30	88·3	(730)	91·2	(1,732)	94·2	(2,615)	96·0	(1,248)
30·1–50	92·6	(128)	91·8	(698)	94·1	(617)	94·5	(83)
> 50	89·5	(203)	91·8	(178)	98·5	(26)	—	

The discussion of the impact of social characteristics on performance can be extended by including an examination of the general social and community characteristics of the school neighbourhood (i.e. an index of social deprivation). This was developed by the ILEA (and it included measures of economic and housing stress, teacher and pupil turnover, as well as measures of immigrant concentration and social composition which are important here). Table 6.5 presents the variation in performance when schools are grouped by scores on an EPA index, but owing to the small numbers in some sub-groups the analysis is presented for non-manual and manual groups and not for each occupational group separately. Among children from non-manual backgrounds, none of the differences shown is statistically significant, and, more important, there is no clear trend such as has emerged in previous tables, except possibly in the lowest priority group (4). However, it should be noted that in the third priority group (3) there is a trend but it is in the *opposite direction*, i.e. performance appears to improve with increasing immigrant concentration. For the high-priority groups there is no clear pattern. Further, it can be seen from table 4 that the general indicator of social and educational problems is a more important factor than simply that of immigrant concentration. This can be deduced from the fact that in nearly all sub-groups the mean scores of children in a low-priority group are higher than those of children in a higher priority group, whatever the immigrant concentration. For example, the mean score of children in priority group (2) in predominantly immigrant schools is 99.1, as compared with a mean of 97·5 of those in schools of less than 10 per cent immigrants but in priority group (1). Among the manual children such trends as there are would seem to point towards high performance being related to high immigrant concentration. In summary it would seem from this analysis that when account is taken of other factors, in particular parental occupation and the school's educational priority rank, the factor of immigrant concentration is of negligible importance in determining non-immigrants' performance.

Fewer West Indians (who account for half the immigrants in the survey B) are in schools of low immigrant concentration and more in schools of high concentration than 'other' immigrants. This is important, since West Indians perform on average much less well than the 'other' immigrants. For this reason it was necessary to carry out the analysis for each nationality group separately. However, the resulting numbers in some sub-groups were so small that many of the tables presenting only the West Indians and 'other' immigrants have been included. Among West Indians, Greek Cypriots and Indians attainment is very similar, regardless of immigrant concentration, with the exception that there is a lower attainment in schools with over 60 per cent immigrants. Among the Pakistanis and Turkish Cypriots there is no clear pattern, but the differences between sub-groups are much larger. However, the numbers of children involved are small and no clear trend is discernible. Among the 'other' immigrants there appears to be a trend similar to that shown for the non-immigrants, i.e. declining attainment with increasing immigrant concentration. However, this trend appears to be reversed in the group of 50–60 per cent immigrants (see table 6.6).

TABLE 6.6

Mean reading score of immigrant children classified by nationality in schools of varying immigrant concentration

Percentage of immigrants	West Indian	Indian	Pakistani	Greek Cypriot	Turkish Cypriot	Other
< 10	88·1 (228)	90·5 (48)	90·7 (26)	86·8 (63)	87·1 (32)	96·0 (236)
10·1–20	89·1 (401)	90·2 (70)	92·1 (43)	86·4 (81)	85·5 (48)	93·1 (256)
20·1–30	87·3 (364)	89·8 (48)	94·3 (33)	88·7 (100)	82·2 (39)	94·1 (173)
30·1–40	87·4 (343)	89·6 (33)	87·3 (15)	85·6 (51)	84·3 (73)	91·3 (120)
40·1–50	88·0 (203)	89·9 (15)	83·1 (7)	86·1 (22)	79·2 (25)	86·5 (43)
50·1–60	87·6 (330)	87·9 (14)	88·3 (9)	85·6 (50)	81·5 (30)	93·3 (54)
60·1–70	84·7 (57)	75·4 (8)	78·7 (6)	88·5 (14)	81·3 (17)	85·1 (14)

Against the effect of the general social characteristics of the school and the area need examining, and tables 6.7 and 6.8 show their impact on West Indian and other immigrant pupils. The most significant point in table 6.7 is the small differences in mean scores between the sub-groups. It does not matter whether one reads across or down the table (varying priority rank or immigrant concentration); differences are small. The largest difference is of only six points. Furthermore it is not possible to discern any clear trend; in schools of the highest and

TABLE 6.7

Mean reading score of West Indian children in schools of varying immigrant concentration and educational priority

Percentage of immigrants	Educational priority rank							
	1		2		3		4	
< 10	85·1	(19)	85·6	(52)	87·5	(81)	89·9	(107)
10·1–30	86·5	(110)	86·1	(279)	87·7	(370)	90·7	(172)
30·1–50	84·5	(72)	86·2	(271)	88·2	(273)	88·7	(27)
> 50	84·3	(197)	87·8	(214)	90·9	(34)		

TABLE 6.8

Mean reading score of 'other' immigrants in schools of varying immigrant concentration and education priority ranking

Percentage of immigrants	Educational priority rank							
	1		2		3		4	
< 10			89·8	(19)	90·8	(53)	97·6	(174)
10·1–30	92·1	(34)	90·7	(93)	92·9	(182)	95·2	(162)
30·1–50	82·6	(30)	88·2	(53)	89·4	(75)	104·6	(19)
> 50	88·3	(27)	92·0	(38)	94·0	(7)		

lowest priority there is no trend, and in schools of the two middle priority groups there is a *slight* trend of increased attainment with increased concentration, and if anything the pattern appears to be less clear among the 'other' immigrants. The differences shown in table 6.8 are in fact greater than those among West Indians, being in some cases as much as ten points. However, the only difference which is statistically significant is that in the highest priority group between children in schools of 10–30 per cent immigrants and those in schools of 30–50 per cent immigrants: 92·1 as compared with 82·6. Furthermore in no priority group is a clear trend discernible. Finally, for the 'other' immigrants (unlike the West Indians) education priority rank would seem to be an important factor. The differences between some sub-groups are large: for example, there is a range of twenty-two points between children in schools of 30–50 per cent immigrant concentration as between the lowest and highest priority schools.

In conclusion it would seem that with the exception of very high and very low concentration there is no evidence to support the hypothesis that non-immigrant (or immigrant) children are adversely affected in their reading attainment by being taught in a school of varying immigrant concentration, nor conversely is immigrant children's attainment higher if they are taught in a school of low immigrant concentration. Compared with parental occupation and the index of multiple deprivation (education priority rank), the factor of immigrant concentration would appear to be of small and inconsistent importance. Children in high-concentration immigrant schools are likely, however, to attain at a lower level than their peers because they are more likely also to come from a less advantaged home background and—regardless of immigrant concentration—the school is more likely to be a disadvantaged school. More specifically the following points emerge from survey B:

1   ILEA junior schools present considerable variety in the degree of both social and ethnic mix. Something like 40 per cent of ILEA pupils are in schools with a social or immigrant concentration comparable (within 10 per cent limits) to the authority as a whole. About a quarter of middle-class children are in predominantly middle-class schools (i.e. 50 per cent or more middle-class), nearly a half of all lower working-class children are in schools which are predominantly lower working-class (50 per cent or more), while a sixth of the immigrant children are in predominantly immigrant schools (50 per cent or more).

2   The effect of immigrant concentration on educational performance is less important than the degree to which schools are experiencing multiple deprivation. As far as immigrant children are concerned, their performance is only marginally affected by the immigrant concentration in the school. Non-immigrant children appear to be affected at the extremes of concentration: children in schools with less than 10 per cent immigrants have a reading age approximately one year in advance of those children in schools with over

60 per cent immigrants. However, the variation between these extremes is slight: children in schools of between 10 and 50 per cent immigrants attain at very much the same level. Moreover the relationship between immigrant concentration and performance is complicated by the fact that children in schools of low immigrant concentration come from predominantly higher-status occupational backgrounds and the schools are furthermore low on the index of multiple deprivation, whereas children in high-concentration schools are predominantly working-class and the schools are high on the index of multiple deprivation.

3   When social and ethnic mix appear to be closely related to performance it is at a level which an explicit policy directed towards encouraging and supporting such social and ethnic mix could not achieve in an area with a large number of recent settlers. For example, immigrant proportions of less than 10 per cent cannot be achieved in an authority in which the overall percentage of immigrants is twice that.

4   We are confronted, then, by a situation in which no matter how desirable for other social and educational reasons social and ethnic mix may be, it cannot be justified in terms of the performance measures used in this paper. Either the gains are too small to warrant the policy effort or the objectives are unrealistic in terms of the characteristics of the population. Improved educational performance by underprivileged children might be achieved if appropriate action were taken based on an examination of the social and psychological dynamics which underpin the index of multiple deprivation referred to in this paper and the mobilisation of suitable resourcee to alleviate the situation. This conclusion should not be allowed to deflect attention from the minority of children in highly atypical school situations, especially when such extreme concentrations are deviant not simply from the authority or borough population but from smaller, more local areas. Nor to the possibility of encouraging dispersal out of areas of heavy concentration (for example, two out of three West Indians are in the Greater London area) into other parts of the country. Again, whether larger gains could be achieved by a policy directed towards greater social and ethnic mix, or by national,

regional and local policies of positive discrimination in educational resources towards the disadvantaged schools is at least debatable. The pay-off in terms of educational attainment of greater mix is perhaps indicated in this paper and may be small. How far dramatic redistribution and proper utilisation of scarce educational resources would have a more significant impact is not known, but such a policy is consistent with the strong influence shown in this paper of 'multiple deprivation' on attainment.

TABLE 6.9

Performance of immigrant and non-immigrant pupils by class and ethnic concentration of school

	English		Mathematics		Verbal reasoning	
	% 1 + 2	% 6 + 7	% 1 + 2	% 6 + 7	% 1 + 2	% 6 + 7
Immigrants						
1 Percentage of immigrants in school:						
< 10%	9·5	47·4	9·9	44·6	8·0	52·6
10–49%	8·4	54·5	8·4	54·7	7·2	59·8
>50%	6·0	50·4	5·3	54·6	3·6	59·6
Non-immigrants						
1 Percentage of immigrants in school:						
< 10%	27·9	20·4	25·9	22·6	22·9	25·8
10–49%	23·9	24·4	21·1	26·4	18·6	30·0
> 50%	18·0	30·7	14·3	33·9	12·7	37·3
Immigrants						
2 Percentage semi-unskilled in neighbourhood:						
0–49%	11·5	47·2	11·4	47·0	9·3	52·4
50–59%	5·3	56·4	4·9	58·8	4·3	63·5
> 60%	5·9	57·3	6·2	57·5	5·3	63·3
Non-immigrants						
2 Percentage semi-unskilled in neighbourhood:						
0–49%	29·1	19·9	27·2	21·6	23·7	24·7
50–59%	20·7	24·0	17·1	27·8	15·1	30·1
> 60%	21·7	27·8	20·0	29·7	16·9	33·7

These conclusions are so important that it is worth looking at survey (A) in a similar way to see whether it is consistent with these results. When the percentage of immigrants in schools was related to performance (see table 6.9) the distribution of immigrants' performance was closest to non-immigrants in schools with less than 10 per cent immigrants, though even these distributions had a negative bias when compared with actual ILEA distributions. The distributions of those in schools with 10–19 per cent immigrants were slightly more negatively biased than those of the 0–10 per cent immigrant roll schools, but the first marginal drop in performance came for those in schools with 20–29 per cent and 30–39 per cent immigrant concentration. Performance improved to about the level of those in 10–19 per cent roll schools for those in schools with 40–49 per cent immigrants but dropped sharply for those in schools with 50–59 per cent immigrants, to 'level off' for schools with 60 per cent immigrants or more. These differences in performance based on immigrant concentration remained when different patterns of length of stay or nationality of pupils in schools were controlled. It is important to remember that the differences discussed here are in English, mathematics and verbal reasoning.

There was greater variance in performance based on immigrant concentration for the non-immigrants than for the immigrants. When non-immigrants in schools with no immigrants are included for comparison, the pattern which emerged was one of very high performance amongst non-immigrants in schools with no immigrants and slightly less good performance in schools with 0–10 per cent immigrants; an identifiable drop in performance for those in schools with 10–19 per cent immigrants (but no differences between those groups and schools with 20–29, 30–39, 40–49 percentages)—though performance was still better than the actual ILEA. This is followed by two large drops in performance for those in schools with 50–59 per cent and 60 per cent or more immigrants. The largest differences in performance were in the 'extreme' schools (those with either no immigrants at all or those with over 50 per cent immigrant rolls), non-immigrant pupils in the former having distribution superior to the rest of the authority, non-immigrants in the latter having distributions inferior to the remainder of the Authority. When immigrants and non-immigrants in the same schools (controlling both the immigrant and class composition of the school) were compared, in no instance did the immigrants do as well as the non-immigrants. However, the performance of certain groups (long-stay Asian immigrants) was at least equal to the indigenous population.

Concerning the relative importance of percentage immigrant roll and concentration of working class in determining performance:

1 For both immigrants and non-immigrants the 'social' composition of the neighbourhood seems to account for more of the differences in performance than did the immigrant composition of the schools.

2 Immigrant composition seems to be an important influence on the immigrant and non-immigrant performance when the percentage of immigrants reaches 50 per cent, and although such situations are not frequent they are the ones in which a formal or informal dispersal policy might have effect.

3 Having no immigrants or very few (less than 10 per cent) seems to be related to relatively high levels of performance for both immigrants and non-immigrants but as the percentage increases from 10 to 19, 20 to 29, 30 to 39 and 40 to 49 only slight and sometimes inconsistent changes occur. There is some evidence that the increases affect non-immigrant more than immigrant performance. But low immigrant proportion was closely related to low working-class concentration of the neighbourhood, and it is therefore related to the interaction of social and ethnic mix.

A comparison of immigrant school performance with underprivileged indigenous children (source: survey C). The comparison of immigrant and non-immigrant performance within the same category of school is worth examining with reference to the reading ages found in project B. Table 6.10 gives the mean reading scores for non-immigrants from semi and unskilled working-class backgrounds and for West Indians. All the comparisons suggest the West Indians in similar school categories are performing at a lower level than the underprivileged white pupils, and this finding is confirmed by the EPA study (project C). The mean reading standards of all pupils on the SRA test was nine points (nearly one year in reading age) below the national mean: the

96   A. N. LITTLE

TABLE 6.10

Mean reading score of lower working-class and West Indian pupils, by immigrant concentration

Percentage of immigrants in school	Semi-skilled	Unskilled	West Indian
−10	94·5	91·9	88·1
−30	92·9	89·8	88·0
−50	92·8	89·7	87·6
50+	93·1	87·6	87·2

mean score of non-immigrants was 93·4, that of West Indians 89·4 points and that of other immigrants 90 points. Within the area defined as 'underprivileged' the indigenous pupils' mean reading achievement was four points above that of the West Indian settler pupil population.

Confirmation of the same points can be obtained from the analysis of the English Picture Vocabulary Test (see table 6.11). This test has

TABLE 6.11

Score of pupils on the EPVT in EPA schools

	Level 1			Level 2		
	N	Mean	SD	N	Mean	SD
All pupils	1341	94·5	14·8	1551	90·9	13·8
Non-immigrant	957	97·9	13·8	1162	92·9	13·0
West Indian	298	86·9	12·8	250	85·5	13·1

two levels, one for infant school pupils (level 1) and the other for pupils in the junior age range (level 2). Several interesting points emerge from this analysis. Pupils in schools defined as EPA score over five points below the national norm on level 1 and nine points below on level 2. West Indians in infant schools (and therefore pupils who are likely to have a full United Kingdom education in the future) scoring thirteen points below their national age peers and eleven points below their indigenous classmates. In junior schools the gap between them and their national age peers is nearly fifteen points and with class peers over seven points. What stands out is that even at a very young age (i.e. in infant schools) the indigenous white pupil in an EPA school is performing at a significantly higher level than his black classmate but at a significantly lower level than his national age peer. It is worth noting that this finding is confirmed by a study completed in another EPA area using the pre-school version of the English Picture Vocabulary Test: sixty-three non-immigrants in the area (mean age of four years five months) had a standardised score of 95·2, twenty-three immigrants (mean age four years seven months) a standardised score of 84·1. This indicates that the gap in passive vocabulary pre-dates school entry.

The English Picture Vocabulary Test is a test of passive vocabulary. As a broader measure of language skills the study used the Illinois Test of Psycholinguistic Abilities. The test was administered individually to a sample of classes with second-year junior pupils in some of the EPA schools. The test was used as part of a language programme evaluation to draw a psycho-linguistic profile of the language skills of EPA children. Unfortunately it had no English norms. Detailed results are given in table 6.12 but three main general

TABLE 6.12

Mean scores on individual items on the ITPA

		Non-immigrant	West Indian	Other immigrant
1*	Auditory reception	30·7	23·9	26·8
2	Visual reception	21·0	20·6	23·3
3*	Auditory association	26·9	24·5	23·7
4	Visual association	23·6	21·3	22·2
5*	Verbal expression	31·0	27·4	27·3
6	Manual expression	28·5	27·1	24·3
7*	Grammatical closure	28·0	18·4	19·0
8	Visual closure	25·0	22·3	22·0
9*	Auditory memory	30·9	32·4	27·5
10	Visual memory	20·1	18·5	18·5
	N	101	27	6

findings are significant. When considering these results the small numbers of pupils involved in this aspect of the project must be remembered (i.e. 101 non-immigrants, twenty-seven West Indians and six other immigrants).

1   The overall 'psycho-linguistic profile' of the group of children tested was below and different from American norms. On the information available it is impossible to attribute this to differences between groups of English and American children or between normal English and English EPA groups of children.
2   Relative to the other areas of their psycho-linguistic functioning, EPA children appear to have perception difficulties (i.e. they have difficulty deriving meaning from stimuli presented to them either visually or orally); on the other hand they seem to have little difficulty in expressing themselves either verbally or manually.
3   The West Indian sub-group of children have a 'psycho-linguistic profile' which is different from that of non-immigrant EPA children when the auditory vocal channel of communication is being used. Half the ten IPTA sub-tests concentrate on skills involving this communication channel (those marked with an asterisk 12); on four of them West Indian children had significantly different and lower scores than their non-immigrant EPA classmates. On sub-tests involving the other communication channel tested on the IPTA—the visual–motor channel—there was no significant difference between the non-immigrant and West Indian groups. On one of the sub-tests involving the auditory–vocal channel (the Grammatic Closure Test) West Indian children had particularly different scores from the non-immigrant group.

These findings confirm many teacher statements about West Indian children; namely that they are deficient in areas where language must be used as a directive tool but when visual–motor skills are necessary their performance is not different from their non-immigrant peers, and, combined with the EPVT finding (the passive vocabulary of the immigrant groups was significantly smaller than that of non-immigrant groups), provide a starting point for developing teaching programmes designed to meet the special needs of West Indian pupils.

A final series of data is available from project C. One of the main curriculum schemes was an environmental studies exercise for fourth-year junior pupils in the EPA schools. As part of this evaluation the Bristol Achievements Tests were used (which gave pupil performance in English, mathematics and study skills). Table 6.13 summarises the scores of pupils at the beginning of the project: on English the indigenous pupils scored over eight points below the standardised scores and West Indian pupils over twelve points below. On mathematics the

TABLE 6.13

Mean standard score of EPA pupils on Bristol Achievement Tests

	Non-immigrants (N = 202)	West Indians (N = 54)	Other immigrants (N = 21)
English	91·5	87·6	86·8
Study skills	93·2	86·5	85·2
Mathematics	96·9	91·00	88·1

difference was three points and nine points, on study skills nearly seven points for the indigenous and over thirteen points for West Indians. Children of new settlers in this country are performing at a level (on English, mathematics and study skills) not only below their age peers in the rest of the country but below the indigenous under-privileged children in EPA schools

The main results of these comparisons and their implications for education

Four main results stand out:

1   The immigrant pupulation is differentiated in terms of its adjustment to the performance in the English education system. Of the two main groups of New Commonwealth settlers (Asians and West Indians), the Asians appear to be performing at a higher level than the West Indians.
2   Length of education in the United Kingdom appears to be a more important factor in determining primary school performance than length of residence or being born in the country. But even with full

education the performance of pupils from certain backgrounds is
below that of the indigenous population.

3   With the exception of extremes, the social and ethnic mix of the
school appears to have little influence on the performance of
either the indigenous or the settler population. Where it does have
an effect (where there are very few or very many settlers) it
appears to influence the privileged pupils more than the underprivileged (middle-class rather than working-class, white rather
than black). Further, positive gains in performance take place at a
level of minority and class composition outside the possibility of
policy changes in areas of heavy settlement.

4   The relatively poor performance of minority pupils is across the
curriculum (passive and active vocabulary, verbal reasoning,
reading, English, mathematics and study skills), although some
differences can be found in certain parts of the curriculum.
Finally underprivileged white children perform at a higher level
than West Indian settlers, and this appears to be true of pupils
before and in the early years of their primary education.

It is important to clarify what these broad generalisations mean. They
refer to the relative performance of various sections of the population.
Of course many children from minority backgrounds are performing
at a level above that of many children of the indigenous population,
and differences within groups are far greater than that between groups.
Just as the educational system has in a sense failed to meet the needs
of the child from a working-class background, so now, to an even
greater extent, it is failing to meet the needs of the child from a
different cultural background, and this is demonstrated by differences
in mean levels of attainment. Various reasons can be advanced for
these differences. The comparative newness to the United Kingdom
educational system of certain groups is one, the educational consequences of social deprivation and the effects of cultural differences
between minority and majority population are others. However, it is
the inability (or unwillingness) of the existing system to modify its
practice to meet the needs of new types of pupils that should be
stressed. There are two reasons for emphasising the importance of
modifying the existing school system. First, what goes on in school is
a factor determining differences in performance, and second (and

perhaps more important) is the fact that educational policy and practice are under the control of educational policy makers, whereas the other factors are not. Therefore it is suggested that what is required is a careful and critical examination of current educational practice and its modification as a means of improving the levels of achievement reached.

In particular these five implications for action need emphasising:

1 It is the child from the West Indian background whose needs in terms of basic skill performance should be given highest priority. Further indications of some of the differences can be detected at or before school entrance.

2 Without positive action these needs are unlikely to be seriously reduced in the short run: neither being born here nor having a full education brings performance levels up to the indigenous population's. As a higher proportion of pupils from minority home backgrounds are born in the United Kingdom, so the mean levels of performance will improve, but certain sub-groups will continue in the immediate future to be below the indigenous population and even socially disadvantaged white groups.

3 Changing the social and ethnic mix of schools (i.e. bussing or dispersal) in areas of minority settlement is unlikely to change the performance of minority pupils, with the possible exception of basic training in English for non-English speaking pupils.

4 The need for early intervention into development (certainly at the beginning of infant schools and more desirably earlier) of minority pupils.

5 The need to develop programmes specially designed to meet the disadvantages (and particularly the language needs) of children from the West Indian backgrounds, and to expand language programmes for pupils from non-English-speaking backgrounds.

Bibliography

Acland, H. (1972) 'Social determinants of educational achievement: an evaluation and criticism of research.' PhD thesis, Oxford University.

Ainsworth, M. E. and Batten, E. J. (1974) *The Effects of Environmental Factors on Secondary Educational Attainment in Manchester: a Plowden Follow-up.* Schools Council Research Studies. London: Macmillan.

Anderson, B. B. and Hansene, J. (1972) 'Foraeldre og skole.' *Study 25.* Copenhagen: Danish National Institute of Social Research.

Batten, E. J. (1974) 'A study of the relationship between some home environment variables and secondary school achievement'. PhD thesis, Manchester University.

Benn, C. and Simon, B. (1970) *Half-way there.* Harmondsworth: Penguin Books.

Bereiter, C. and Engleman, C. (1966) *Teaching Disadvantaged Children in the Pre-school.* Englewood Cliffs, N.J.: Prentice-Hall.

Bernstein, B. (1961) 'Social class and linguistic development: a theory of social learning.' *Education, Economy and Society,* ed. A. H. Halsey *et al.,* pp. 288–314. New York: Free Press.

Burt, C. (1937) *The Backward Child.* London: University of London Press.
—— (1955) 'The evidence for the concept of intelligence.' *Brit. J. Educ. Psychol.* XXV, pp. 158–77.

Bynner, J. M. (1972) *Parents' Attitudes to Education.* London: HMSO.

Byrne, D. S. and Williamson, L. (1972) 'Intra-regional variations in educational provision and their bearing upon educational attainment.' *Sociology* VI.

Chazan, M. (1973) *Compensatory Education.* London: Butterworth.

Cloward, R. A. and Jones, J. A. (1963) 'Social class, educational attitudes and participation.' *Education in Depressed Areas*, ed. A. H. Passow. New York: Columbia University Press.

Community Relations Commission (1974) *Educational Needs of Children from Minority Groups*. London: HMSO.

Donnison, D. (1972) *A Pattern of Disadvantage*. Slough: National Foundation for Educational Research.

Douglas, J. W. B. (1968) *All our Future*. London: Peter Davies.

Floud, J., Halsey, A. H. and Martin, F. M. (1957) *Social Class and Educational Opportunity*. London: Heinemann.

Floud, J. (1961) 'Social class factors in educational achievement.' *Ability and Educational Opportunity*, ed. A. H. Halsey. London: OECD.

—— (1962) 'Teaching in an affluent society.' *Brit. J. Sociol.*

Glennerster, H. (1972) 'Education and inequality.' *Labours and Inequality*, ed. M. Townsend and R. Bosanquet. London: Fabian Society.

Hall, W. (1974) 'Parental involvement and the remedial teaching of reading.' M. Ed. thesis, Manchester University.

Halsey, A. H. (1972) *Educational Priority*, Vols. I–IV, EPA Problems and Politics. London: HMSO.

Haynes, J. (1971) *Educational Assessment of Immigrant Pupils*. Slough: NFER.

Jackson, B., and Marsden, D. (1962) *Education and the Working Class*. London: Routledge & Kegan Paul.

Jencks, C., *et al.* (1972) *Inequality*. London: Allen Lane.

Kellmer-Pringle, M. L, Butler, N. R. and Dane, R. (1966) *Eleven Thousand Seven-year-olds grow up*. London: Longman.

Kelsall, R. K. and H. M. (1971) *Social Disadvantage and Educational Opportunity*. London: Holt Rinehart & Winston.

Lewis, O. (1966) 'The culture of poverty.' *Scientific American*, 215, 4, 19–25.

Little, A. N. and Mabey, C. (1973) 'Reading attainment and social and ethnic mix of London primary schools'. *London Urban Patterns, Problems and Policies*, ed. Donnison and Eversley. London: Heinemann.

Midwinter, E. (1973) *Priority Education*. Harmondsworth: Penguin Books.

Morton-Williams, R. (1967) 'Survey among parents of primary school children,' appendix 3 of the Plowden report, Vol. 2. London: HMSO.

Newsom, J. (1963) *Half our Future*. Central Advisory Council for Education, London: HMSO.

Peaker, G. F. (1967) 'The regression analysis of the national survey,' appendix 4 of the Plowden report, Vol. 2. London: HMSO.

Peters, R. S. (ed.) (1969) *Perspectives on Plowden*. London: Routledge & Kegan Paul.

Pidgeon, D. A. (1970) *Expectations and Pupil Performance*. Slough: NFER.

Plowden report (1967) *Children and their Primary Schools*. London: HMSO.

Rushton, J. and Young, M. (1974) 'Elements of elaboration in working-class writing.' *Educational Research*, XVI, 181–8.

Statistics of Education, Vol. 1. Published annually by the DES. London: HMSO.

Swift, D. F. (1966) 'Social class and achievement motivation.' *Educational Research*, VIII, 83–95.

—— (1968), 'Social class and educational adaptation.' *Education Research in Britain*, ed. H. J. Butcher, I. London: University of London Press.

Taylor, G., and Ayres, N. (1969) *Born and Bred Unequal*. London: Longman.

Teacher Education for a Multi-cultural Society (1974) Community Relations Commission.

The Extent of Racial Discrimination, XL. Broadsheet No. 547, Political and Economic Planning. London: HMSO.

Townsend, H. E. R. and Brittan, E. (1974) *Teacher Education for a Multi-cultural Society*. Slough: NFER.

Turner, R. H. (1961) 'Modes of social ascent through education: sponsored and contest mobility'. *Education, Economy and Society*, ed. A. H. Halsey, J. Floud and Anderson. New York: Free Press.

Will, E. and Vatter, H. G. (1965) *Poverty in Affluence*. New York: Harcourt Brace.

Wiseman, S. (1970) *The Plowden Report*, Vol. 2. London: HMSO.

—— (1964) *Education and Environment*. Manchester University Press.

AUTHOR INDEX

Acland, H., 27, 30
Ainsworth, M. E., 23, 29
Aristotle, 59
Ayres, N., 39

Barnes, J., 48
Batten, E. J., 7, 32
Benn, C., 40
Bereiter, C., 3
Bernstein, B., 5, 52
Burt, C., 27, 31
Bynner, J. M., 5, 7, 27, 30
Byrne, D. S., 27, 39

Chazan, M., 22
Clegg, A., 51
Cloward, R. A., 30
Cuisenaire, G., 63

Dienes, Z. P., 63
Donnison, D., 6
Douglas, J. W. B., 7

Engleman, C., 3

Floud, J., 7, 24

Glennester, H., 44
Gouldner, D., 28

Hall, W., 3
Halsey, A. H., 5, 7, 22, 23, 40, 46, 59,
    60, 68, 72

Jackson, B., 19
Jencks, C., 5, 24, 25

Jones, A., 30
Joseph, K., 57, 60

Kelsall, H. M., 21
Kelsall, R. K., 21

Lewis, O., 2
Little, A. N., 71, 73, 80

Mabey, C., 80
Marsden, D., 19
Martin, F., 7
Midwinter, E., 3, 5, 23, 51, 55, 58
Morris, H., 52
Morrison, H., 67

Newsom, J., 39

Payne, J., 48
Peaker, G. F., 8, 9, 20, 27, 28
Pidgeon, D. A., 8
Plowden, B., 8, 9, 20, 23, 24, 25, 46, 51
    56, 57
Pringle, M. K., 3, 7

Rushton, J., 1, 5

Simon, B., 40
Swift, D. F., 5, 20, 21

Taylor, G., 39
Thatcher, M., 55, 56, 57
Townsend, H. E. R., 72
Turner, R. H., 41

Vatter, H. G., 2

Will, E., 2
Williamson, W., 29
Wiseman, S., 25, 27, 31
Wood, A. J., 55

Young, G. M., 5